BUY ME!

BUY ME!

NEW WAYS TO GET CUSTOMERS TO CHOOSE YOUR
PRODUCTS AND IGNORE THE REST

MARSHAL COHEN

New York   Chicago   San Francisco   Lisbon   London
Madrid   Mexico City   Milan   New Delhi   San Juan
Seoul   Singapore   Sydney   Toronto

1 2 3 4 5 6 7 8 9 0   DOC/DOC   0 1 0 9

ISBN: 978-0-07-166783-8
MHID: 0-07-166783-0

McGraw-Hill books are available at special quantity discounts to use as premiums and sales promotions, or for use in corporate training programs. To contact a representative please e-mail us at bulksales@mcgraw-hill.com.

CONTENTS

v

CONTENTS

CONTENTS

INTRODUCTION

In my previous book, *Why Consumers Do What They Do*, which was published by McGraw-Hill in 2006, I wrote, "I have seen more changes in consumer purchasing behavior in the last two years than I have in the last two decades." Now, upon the publication of *Buy Me!* in 2010, I feel impelled to modify that statement a tad, to the following: I have seen more changes in consumer purchasing behavior in the last two years than I have in my entire *lifetime*.

Indeed, the world is at the brink of a new era of consumption, a time to seek change, to discover new sales strategies, to establish new traditions. The time has come for companies to reach out to their consumers in a whole new way, with rejuvenated methods of communication and product messaging. Nowadays, companies have to reconfigure the timing of their product releases—and time them *right*. Managers, CEOs, salespeople, marketers, and consultants alike now need to approach their businesses with an entirely new set of rules and measurements. Retailers and manufacturers must now adapt to their consumers—and not just sit back and expect their consumers to adapt to *them*. This is the time. This is *your* time.

Sure, you might long for the good old days of consumption, when consumers would stumble upon a product, decide that, yes, they do in fact desire it, and then purchase it without regard for how or when they would pay for it. But those days, the days of conspicuous consumption, are gone—at least for now. To be sure, were you to step back from the retail marketplace for a moment and consider the trends that are driving consumption today, you would find that they are coursing in a direction that runs far afield of even the most time-honored of businesses' realms of experience. Think about it: have you ever been faced with the task of selling to consumers who think twice about every single purchase they might make? That's right: *Every. Single. One.* Or what about consumers who question whether those items that they previously deemed to be necessities are actually needed? Have you ever had to sell to *them*? My guess is: probably not. But like it or not, consumers of today are *not* the consumers of yesterday. No, today's consumers are seeking better prices, better values, and better-timed purchases. They are watching out for new places to shop and fresh ways to do so. They are relying upon their tried-and-true sources of buying advice, like their friends and family, but they are also placing their confidence in online product reviews posted by complete strangers. They are purchasing based on need, not on desire. They are buying for the here and now, not for the future. In short, they are changing *all the rules*.

No matter whether you sell your products to consumers directly or indirectly, whether you sell them a service or a luxury, or whether you sell them fishing line or high-tech electronics, you need to understand, adapt to, and live by the new rules of consumption. And don't think that you can merely wait for the tide of consumer change to pass and then run out, guns ablaze, as soon as consumers are ready to revert back to their old ways of spending. The truth of the matter is that the new era of consumer frugality is deeply rooted, as are its accompanying rules. In fact, there is no guarantee that consumers *ever* will spend in the same manner that they once did. So, take advantage of the information that floods the pages of this book. Give it a read-through. Flip from chapter to chapter, and discover just how much there is to learn about the new era of consumption that is dawning over the sky of retail. And don't forget to fasten your seatbelt: you're in for a wild ride.

BUY ME!

PART 1

THE NEW ECONOMY

CHAPTER | 1

The Age of Thrift

How aware are you of these terms?

- Frugal fatigue
- Pent-up demand
- False wealth
- Great Compression
- Conspicuous consumption
- Necessity vs. desirous spending
- New retail rules
- Consumption coma

You need to be. In order to survive in the "new" world today, you need to understand the dynamics of the second most dramatic shift in consumer behavior in modern times. The combination of Great Depression and the growth that followed it resulted in the most massive shift in consumer behavior that history has ever seen. And now, we are caught in the tide of a shift of lesser, though still significant, proportions: the Great Compression of 2009.

While I think the Great Depression is, by now, something about which most people share a collective knowledge, the Great Compression is not. I define it as: The simultaneous squeeze in pricing, the housing market, and the credit market, all of which act together to put the squeeze on the consumer. Lest we forget, consumer spending makes up about 70 percent—almost three-quarters—of our economy, according to some estimates.

While the current Great Compression is by no means comparable in size or scale to the Great Depression, we can't dismiss the fact that we are witnessing the most dramatic change in consumer behavior in decades. After almost 11 years of amazing, consumer-driven economic growth, the fall has come. I don't think this fall is all that bad, mind you. We have been living on both borrowed time and borrowed money, and it was all but inevitable that the end would come and our bloated economy would get the cleansing it so sorely needed.

As the world celebrated the new millennium, Americans enjoyed continued growth in its economy. There was one major interruption, on September 11, 2001, but Americans showed their amazing resilience and recovered quickly. That resilience set Americans right back on the track of unprecedented growth in all areas of consumption—a consumption that knew no boundaries and spread throughout every demographic profile of consumers: the rich, the poor, the young, the old, all ethnicities, and even all regions. They all posted a prolonged period of growth. The momentum of this continued economic growth, however, is what subsequently caused the huge downturn of 2008. Why? We've been living on a climbing roller-coaster. The upward climb was high and steep, and it had to peak sooner or later. And while it is true that everything that goes up must come down . . . it is also true that the higher the peak, the steeper the drop.

In this book we will explore how we plunged into the Great Compression, the changes we will be living with, and how we as business leaders can adapt to and learn from those changes. But perhaps most importantly we will examine how we can turn adversity into opportunities. Yes, there are opportunities all around us. I see them all the time. In fact, I have been working with many management teams over the past year, helping them analyze their businesses and find ways to grow in this challenging market. It is so rewarding to see a company set a new course and focus on moving forward. It resolves to uncover opportunities—and then it actually acts! Consumers benefit, the company benefits, and often careers are made.

This is a time like no other. Companies have opportunities to rise above mediocrity and position themselves above the crowd. Now is when you can easily make your mark in your field. While your competition sits and waits for the economy to recover, you can begin to build your path to the future immediately. Be ready, and be in position to take advantage when the economy rebounds. Even as I write this, the economy already is showing signs of stabilization that will lead to recovery and ultimately growth.

I say to all of you who are stuck: don't be. Get out of the quicksand and take the first step. Don't sit idly by, waiting for someone or something to lead the way. Make a move! Take a step. Even if you need a midcourse correction, you still will be ahead of the competition and poised to take advantage of whatever opportunities the market has for you. So let's go and explore how you can take some key steps that will transform this challenging time into one ripe with opportunities. *Ready?*

LEARNING FROM THE RECENT PAST

In August of 2008 it became very clear that the economic tide had changed. Consumers, believed to be the pillars of the economy (remember they account for 70 percent of our economy), started to show some signs of a change in behavior. In fact, their spending was shifting in huge ways. Due to the enormity of the consumers impact their purchasing behavior was going to become the most important indicator of our economic climate since the dot-com boom went bust.

What I saw back in August 2008, during that all-important back-to-school shopping period, were consumers who were not in a hurry to go out and start spending. They were telling retailers that they needed to be "incentivized" before they would start shopping. They were going to wait until retailers began offering price discounts and other buyers' benefits before they would be convinced to purchase products beyond just the essentials. Gone were the days when consumers would spend freely, without regard for a budget. Consumers' newfound constraint during that back-to-school retail season reflected a major shift in their purchasing priorities. Spending during that back-to-school season showed no growth for the first time in a decade. It became clear to me that consumer behavior was about to shift dramatically, but no one could anticipate just how big that shift would be.

Let's fast-forward just one month, to September 2008, when the lull in retail spending across all industries made it very apparent that we were in the midst of a recession. I recall being on air with Bloomberg Television and speaking with anchor Kathleen Hayes. She asked me what it means when consumers curtail their spending so much that retail is affected across the board. I used the word *recession*. You could hear the entire listening audience gasp. Yes, I really put that word out there. I'll admit, I said it: the "R" word. I told Kathleen that we were in a recession, but that no one wanted to call it that just yet. I recall saying that the government would officially tell us we were in a recession when we hit the second successive quarter of negative growth of gross domestic product (GDP), but that by the time the recession was called, we actually would have been in it for seven months or more. I also recall saying that it would be best if we found out we really were in a recession and began working toward getting out of it.

Kathleen and I continued our on-air conversation, discussing how confident I was that we were in a recession and how we got to this challenged economy in the first place. I reminded Kathleen about what I call "false wealth," the phenomenon created by all those lovely newly formed banks, like Countrywide, that were offering what are now called "liar loans." These institutions were making liar loans to home buyers at 120 percent financing, which in turn brought an average of $60,000 of "spending money" per buyer. This "extra" $60,000 was all "found money." Regardless of whether they had just signed their first mortgage, were trading up, or were trading down, these home buyers were offered money beyond the purchase price of their home with little regard for their income or how they were going to pay it back. Of course, not all home loans were this reckless, but even the more secured loans were offering home buyers the opportunity to borrow more money than they really needed. It seemed like the gift of a lifetime. It was like "free money," and everyone was doing it, so people found themselves asking, "Why not me?" And who could blame them for taking advantage of these loans? After all, they were being advised to take out more money than they needed by "the experts." The banks used so-called liar loans to create a feeding frenzy that even long-term conservative institutions found too attractive to avoid. And when the found money from consumers who were refinancing their homes or signing reverse mortgages was added into the mix, the economy was hit with a double whammy. Suddenly over a quarter of a trillion dollars was injected into retail spending and investing from consumers who just a few years ago barely had two nickels to rub together.

Do the math if you don't believe me. Roughly five hundred thousand newly constructed homes and five hundred thousand existing homes were sold in 2007, totaling approximately 1 million home sales. Now take those 1 million home sales and consider the fact that the average selling price for a home in the United States in 2007 was $300,000. Since 120 percent financing deals were the norm for home purchases made in 2007, figure that each buyer borrowed about 20 percent in extra money—roughly $60,000 per $300,000 home sale (20 percent × $300,000 = $60,000)—against his or her home.

Multiply the average amount of financing per home sale by the number of homes sold in 2007 ($60,000 × 1 million) and you get $60 billion. When you add in all the reverse mortgages and second mortgages that were signed during 2007, you have the potential to reach another 1 million borrowers, which tacks on an additional $60 billion to the mix. We are at $120 billion. Yes, that's $120 billion in just one year. With 120 percent financing being practiced for a few years before the bottom fell out of the real estate market, that $120 billion per year adds up awfully quickly. Between the years of 2003 and 2007, over half a trillion dollars were injected into retail with little regard for its cost, value, and origin, which is why I call this time span "the era of spending with reckless abandon."

WHAT DOES THIS ALL MEAN FOR BUSINESSES?

We've identified that a massive amount of money was introduced to consumers, which they then introduced into the economy. But what happened with this money was not a normal path of consumption. Consumers didn't use the money to pay down their already overleveraged debt. They didn't use it to pay down their mortgages or pay off their other debt. They spent it. They spent it in ways that would reward them. They used it to live more lavish lifestyles. Consumers spent it on higher-end products. They spent this newfound wealth like drunken sailors on shore leave after payday. Consumers were spending the money on home renovations. They purchased big-screen televisions and then decided, hey, why not buy a home theater system? McMansions needed to be furnished and equipped with the latest technology and gadgets. Appliances bearing expensive finishes like stainless steel were soaked up. Or how about those fancy, new, colored washers and dryers that have front loading? The thinking was: let's go out and get one of those, too.

Consumers desired luxury in items as simple as countertops, and so began an upswing in the use of granite or synthetic stone. No Formica for this new crop of homeowners! Formica might have been fine when baby boomers were growing up, but these consumers were concerned about "the resale value" of their homes; therefore the new norm was to install stone countertops and kitchens fit for a celebrity chef. And of course the bathrooms had to be upgraded or built to look like the ones found in a five-star hotel. Nothing less would do. Garages had to have storage systems as wonderful as the cabinetry you'd find in the kitchen. Media rooms had to be outfitted to offer simultaneous viewings of multiple football games on a weekend or equipped to provide the experience of a real movie theater when the latest DVD was popped in for the kids. These luxuries all became must-haves in this new world of conspicuous consumption.

If you consider this trend of consumer behavior and buyers' new fondness for luxury in the contexts of fashion and technology, you will quickly see how we became enmeshed in our conspicuous consumption.

Consumers were able to justify buying designer handbags, first for $300, then for $500, until eventually even $1,000 handbags were okay. The price of jeans rose to over $300, and kids—yes, kids—were able to convince Mom or Dad that they couldn't live without their pair of preference. This was not a new phenomenon. We saw this kind of consumer behavior a decade earlier with athletic shoes, when teens were spending over $100 for basketball shoes in which they had no intention of playing basketball. But it was different this time: it was happening everywhere and with everyone. The notion of "thrift" as a word, concept, or practice was all but extinct. Extravagance became the new norm.

Consumers were driving the economy like never before. Thanks to consumers' exaggerated spending and "false wealth," certain businesses began looking very attractive, prosperous, and successful.

Unfortunately businesses were unaware of just how vulnerable consumers' false wealth was making them. They were relying on consumers that were lacking a proper foundation to support the continuation of their extravagant purchasing behavior. Consumers were driving the economy along, but not for long. Eventually their home loans would have to be adjusted and paid back. This new source of money would dry up. Consumption would drop off. And it surely did.

By the time October 2008 rolled around, with the holiday season rapidly approaching, the consumer was tapped out. The banks had fallen prey to their greed, the housing market dried up, credit stiffly tightened, and consumers lost their Wheel of Fortune. Moms and dads found themselves struggling to figure out how to pay the mortgage, the electric bill, the credit card bills, and a host of other expenses. Households worldwide were faced with the hard truth: there was no more false wealth. And with that, consumers started cutting back—and cutting back fast. Awaiting deals and discounts, parents delayed their back-to-school spending, and in some cases they did not spend at all. Kids were starting the new school year with last year's backpack, some with no or very few new items in their wardrobes.

The new era was upon us. Even still, so few saw the warning light. With a sluggish back-to-school season in 2008, it was easy to predict the consumer spending turnout for the upcoming holiday. I called it "a red Christmas" and a "hesitation holiday." This, I predicted, would be the holiday that spending would be very late in coming and in some cases would barely show up at all. That is exactly what happened. Consumers had adjusted their spending, but by the time retailers' sales figures reflected this shift in consumer behavior, we were already well into the holiday season. Retailers had no time to react to the consumer cutback, which was the first deep decline in U.S. spending in almost a decade. They were committed to their orders, and their inventories were poised for a typical postmillennium holiday season of growth. Even the holiday season of 2001 had posted growth, despite the impact of the events of September 11, so why not now? "After all, just because it was a challenging back-to-school season doesn't mean that we'll be affected now," many retailers believed.

Well, the perfect storm showed up that holiday. The housing market was tanking, credit dried up, consumption slowed to a screeching halt, the consumer all but disappeared, and the retailers had inventories that could choke a horse. (Now, understand, I live on a horse farm, and all that those horses do is eat and graze, morning till night, so enough to choke a horse is a lot!) Inventories were at the optimal level for a normal market, but the market was subpar. The tricky timing of this consumer pullback made it hard for retailers to read. If consumers had cut back any earlier in the year, holiday season inventories would have been adjusted accordingly. But timing wasn't on the retailers' side. So much inventory and so few customers led to discounts of a lifetime. To keep inventory in line, retailers were forced to discount their merchandise at record-breaking levels. Sales with discounts of up to 75 percent off were almost everywhere, and some stores even threw in an additional 25 percent off on top of their already discounted prices in order to move merchandise.

For retailers, the goal became to get whatever revenue you could for your merchandise at any price you could sell it. The thinking was: get inventories in line and generate whatever revenue you can to survive the holiday storm. The 2008 holiday retail season gave consumers the greatest bargains they likely will see in their consumption lifetimes, but not many had the finances to take advantage of the deals.

The events leading up to the Great Compression of 2009 brought about a dramatic change in consumption as we had known it, a change that spread to all income levels as consumers (even those with money) prepared for the other shoe to drop. Their wealth was diminishing right before their eyes, through the declining value of their stock portfolios, their homes, or both. Even the wealthy didn't feel so wealthy. *Consumption as we knew it was about to change in a way that most people had never seen.* Every purchase was scrutinized. Every purchase was evaluated, and if it was not an absolute necessity, it was put off. *Consumers went from spending with reckless disregard to buying necessities only.*

The retail world was not equipped to handle such a dramatic shift in consumer behavior, nor was the manufacturing world. From clothes to cars to electronics to elevators, companies would have to adjust to *less*. Less-than-expected sales, less-than-expected construction, and less need became the new world with which businesses would have to wrestle. Jobs started to fall by the wayside, and alongside the decline in jobs dropped consumer confidence, which reached an all-time low.

We have been tracking consumer spending behavior for over 50 years at NPD. In January 2007, we began analyzing consumers' psyches and asking specific questions about their views on both the state of the economy and the security of their jobs. The purpose of our study was to gauge how consumers were feeling at any given time about the stability of the economy.

NPD launched this study right around the time I began to realize just how much money was being injected into the marketplace through the false wealth phenomenon. My concern was that we, as consumers, were living on a prayer and would not be able to sustain the level of consumption we had reached in 2007. I knew that once consumption began to dwindle, the implications would be far-reaching, so to measure both consumption and the mindset of the consumer, I created a measuring stick and called it the Consumer Spending Indicator. What the Consumer Spending Indicator measured was how comfortable consumers were with the state of the economy, their income, and the security of their jobs. It proved to be a most valuable tool, and it is what enabled me to accurately predict the economic downturn to the exact month of its onset.

As Figure 1.1 shows, consumers' concern about the economy continually increased at a steady pace of almost 3 percent each month. By October 2008, the Consumer Spending Indicator was revealing a big jump in consumer concern, which was reflected at cash registers nationwide. Indeed, October was the first of many months during which the overall retail market began feeling the pain of the brewing Great Compression.

The highs in consumer concern that we reached in October 2008 continued through to December 2008, when our survey respondents indicated that they were significantly concerned again. And like clockwork, once again, the retail market environment was a direct reflection of consumers' concerns.

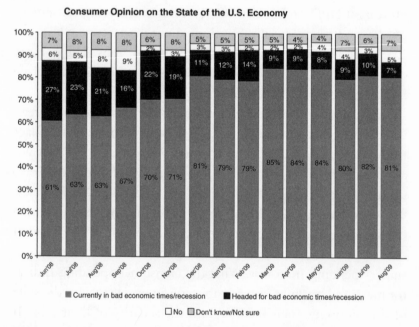

Figure 1.1 NPD's Monthly Consumer Spending Indicator

Now look forward to January and February of 2009, when the Consumer Spending Indicator was showing no real increase in consumer concern (see Figure 1.2). Could it be that consumers' concerns about their incomes, job security, and the state of the economy were lessening?

During one of my monthly appearances on Bloomberg TV, I mentioned that the economy just might have stabilized but that it was truly too soon to call. One or two months don't make a trend, I said, but if consumer concern is still showing a steady line on the Consumer Spending Indicator in March, we actually just might be stabilizing. During this particular TV appearance, I was asked a very intelligent question by Kathleen Hayes: "Is it too soon or could it be the product of a false read to state that stabilization might be upon us?" The key, I told her, was going to be the job market. If the job market and consumers' psyches remained stable for another month, then there would be nothing false about the read. But, I added, the read could in fact be more reflective of a trend of stabilization rather than an actual indicator of stability.

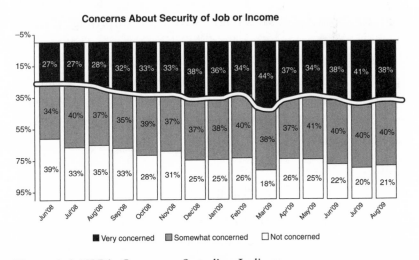

Figure 1.2 NPD's Consumer Spending Indicator

Stability is the first step, a hopeful step, toward recovery. From recovery we could move on to growth. We were all waiting to see if the economy was in fact leveling out, but in March the job market got hit hard, causing responses on the Consumer Spending Indicator to register a greater level of consumer concern. But something odd happened in March. The survey showed that while the percentage of consumers who were deeply concerned about the state of the economy grew, the percentage of consumers who were only somewhat concerned went down by a proportionate amount. The total number of very and somewhat concerned consumers remained level yet again. In spite of the tough job market and a rough month on Wall Street, consumers were showing signs of stability in March 2009. We just needed to look at the situation in a different light.

As I said before, stability is the first hopeful step toward recovery, so after I saw that March 2009 was showing signs of stability, I felt pretty comfortable saying that the economy was going to see a shift in consumption. As April arrived, so did a renewed sales environment at retail. April showed some surprising glimmers of hope that consumers might just be staging their return. Well, the upswing in sales might have been surprising to some, maybe . . . to those people who didn't have the luxury of tracking trends in consumer reporting. According to NPD's Consumer Spending Indicator, consumers were feeling better about the economy, their jobs, and their incomes. Thanks to the Consumer Spending Indicator, April was an easy prediction. The consumer had leveled off.

FRUGAL FATIGUE

It was around April 2009 that I began to see what I call "frugal fatigue." Consumers were beginning to get tired of not being able to buy the things they wanted when they wanted them.

Consumers were beginning to show signs of having a pulse. As frugal fatigue set in, shoppers began loosening their purse strings, shifting from necessity purchasing to replenishment purchasing and buying items they had run out of and thought they could live without. In some cases consumers began replacement purchasing, buying items that were broken or worn instead of opting to repair them. For example, that old washing machine that had kept chugging along with repairs and was in need of another one. The question now was: Do you fix it again or buy a new one? A few months before, there had been no question. The answer was always: repair it. A $150 service call and the cost of the repair were definitely better than buying a new machine in a tough economy.

But, hey, wasn't it only a few short months ago that the consumer didn't hesitate to buy not only a new washer but also a new dryer to go along with it? The stores really incentivized the consumer to do so, offering deals like "buy one appliance and get the second for 20 percent off." Some stores even had deals such as "buy one appliance and get the second for 50 percent off."

But beginning in April 2009, we started to see consumers saying, "Maybe it is a good time to buy that new washer"—or perhaps something else they had been putting off purchasing. Why, you ask? Well, consumers have a very short memory when it comes to being frugal. Just take a look at the price of gas. Remember when gas hit $3 a gallon just awhile back? Car owners' initial reaction was to cut back their driving and rebel against skyrocketing fuel prices, but their frugality lasted all of two months. Let's move forward in time by one year, when prices hit $4 a gallon! Those same drivers stated they would cut back their fuel usage, but did they? Well, not really, and those who did cut back did so for only two months. This is a great example of how quickly we forget, but it's also a great illustration of what I call the "rubber-band effect." Think of a rubber band that is stretched farther than its natural state. Once it is stretched beyond its original size, it will no longer return to its natural state but rather returns to its stretched-out state as a matter of course. It's as though the new stretched-out state is where the rubber band belongs, shifting its natural state so it is now bigger than it was before. In essence, the rubber band adapts to being stretched out.

The rubber-band effect is not limited to just gas prices. Consumers exhibit this behavior when they purchase other items as well. Another example? Just look at premium jean prices. Today, $100 designer jeans don't sound so crazy. But think back to five years ago, when people's heads would have spun at the mere mention of someone paying $100 or more for a pair of premium jeans.

All of this has led to the point at which we find today's consumer: inexorably changed. Consumers are getting used to higher prices and diminished spending power after having been taken to the highest heights of luxury and dropped into the depths of a recession. Although they want to spend, consumers are trying to be more frugal and more thoughtful. It wasn't rising gas prices but rather the economic crisis that caused consumers to drive less and change their consumption behavior for the long term.

HOW TO BENEFIT FROM CONSUMER BEHAVIOR

Now, what's a business to do? It is critical during this rebound period that businesses recognize that the events leading up to the Great Compression of 2009 have dramatically shifted consumption behavior. This means you will need new methods of enticing consumers to purchase your goods. You cannot simply sell to multiple channels like you did just one year ago. Now, you need to persuade consumers to replace that worn-out machine. Forget about repairs. Get them to "invest" in a new product. Look at the situation this way: Almost every year appliance makers, like the auto or fashion industries, update their models, making the previous year's models or styles obsolete. So if you purchase a washer this year and come back in a year or two to replace your dryer, you might find a similar model to the one sitting broken at home, but most likely you are not going to be able to purchase the match that completes your set.

When the economy was humming and lots of false wealth had flooded the marketplace, consumers were happy to update their appliances and spend the money to complete the set. During the boom times, it was an easy sell. Now, however, businesses are facing a whole new set of rules. Consumers need to be wooed differently. Perhaps marketing campaigns should focus on reliability, quality, and technology and offer consumers the opportunity to invest in something today without the penalty of losing their perfect set if they wait until tomorrow to purchase the other half. But will the industry have the patience to endure this approach? I don't think so. Businesses likely will be too risk-averse to change their selling habits and will continue to do what they have been doing for years. They will continue to overinvent new designs or make cosmetic changes to their products in the hopes of enticing consumers to go out and buy the latest models. Sounds a lot like the automobile industry, doesn't it? And we all know how that worked out. Even giving cash incentives didn't sell cars that were "all-new models."

So as we enter the new consumer world, we must recognize that while price is critical, value is even more so. Consumers need an incentive to purchase, and these days, price is not enough.

Economic Distractions

Consumers today are so well informed that they literally are living at a pace that exceeds real time. When the news first hit about the challenges in the real estate market—the birthplace of the economic downturn of 2008–2009—it became quite apparent that the subsequent media onslaught was going to play a huge role in the onset of the recession. And since then, we have become the beneficiaries of multiple news outlets, all of which inform us of minute-by-minute developments in the status of the economy. It wasn't always this way. Not long ago, financial news channels reported on topics like energy cost ratios and the price of crude while reportage on matters like the value of the dollar and the rise and fall of the stock market were left for newspapers, online Web sites, and channels like CNBC and Bloomberg.

But then, all of a sudden, every news channel and news media outlet was talking about gas prices, home sales, and the declining value of the real estate market. It became a daily and, in some cases, even hourly occurrence for casual investors to hear news clips about the declining value of their personal wealth. First the news was focused on the drastic increase in the price of crude, and consumers instantly reacted to the price at the pump. The average consumer couldn't fathom how prices could rise so much so quickly. If it takes seven months from the date of drilling for crude oil to be pumped into the tanks at gas stations, how could the cost of crude affect the price of the gasoline that was already sitting in the tanks at the gas station? Price gouging became a prevalent suspicion for a while, and then came reports that oil companies were posting record profits totaling hundreds of billions of dollars. And even despite their incredible profit gains, oil companies were not letting up on gas prices at the pump. Eventually the price of fuel came down, but not to the same level it had been before.

Here is where the media distractions began. Soon after the media began reporting on rising oil prices and declining home values and housing sales, the stock market started to show some signs of vulnerability. Then the banking industry revealed that an increasing number of banks had been defaulting on their loans, and bank failures subsequently became the subject of the headlines. News about collapsing banks led to talk of government intervention and bailouts. Why some companies were bailed out and others were doomed to bankruptcy became the topic of discussion around many water coolers and lunch tables. President Barack Obama entered office with a score of complicated economic issues he needed to quickly address while the country and the world watched. Then the world markets began to suffer, which drew eyes from all nations to the financial news media. As the economic crisis spread from country to country like a virus, people around the globe became intimately acquainted with just how small the world had become. Almost no one had ever seen or experienced challenges like those that the financial crisis presented. Not only was there no economic growth, but markets worldwide were declining, and consumers could do nothing but watch as their net wealth began to shrink.

These financial news media distractions became addictions, and consumers went into a "consumption coma," second-guessing and overevaluating each and every potential or actual purchase. Then there came an entirely new kind of distraction, this time in the form of anxiety over job security as the job market started to show signs of deterioration. Unemployment numbers began rising steadily and fueled fears of job losses. The quickest way to stop consumption is to let the unemployment numbers climb past 10 percent. At 8 percent we see a major drop off in spending, but at 10 percent fear kicks in *big time*. As you can see from Figure 2.1, U.S. Government data shows that from 2001 to well into 2007, the United States enjoyed uninterrupted job growth.

Figure 2.1 demonstrates that from the turn of the new millennium until late 2007, the United States experienced almost endlessly increasing growth in its job market. It is not normal for job growth to continue uninterrupted for such an extended period of time. It is almost artificial. Economies are healthier when there are ebbs and flows, when the growth rate goes up and down over the course of a few years. The job market is no different. When too much or uninterrupted growth finally is halted, we go from riding a roller-coaster to diving off the side of a cliff. The climb may be high, but the drop is going to be steep.

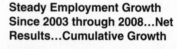

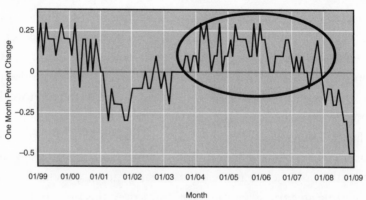

Figure 2.1 U.S. Government Data Showing Steady Employment Growth

Addled by their overexposure to the steadily worsening financial news and their fears for the security of their jobs, consumers began drifting further and further into their consumption comas, which in turn forced retailers and manufacturers into a desperate competition for less and less consumer dollars and interest. In an effort to communicate with these comatose consumers, businesses began launching more advertising, promotions, and marketing campaigns, but their efforts only served to further distract consumers. And the distractions for consumers don't stop there. Add in the fact that consumers' lives have become more and more complex thanks to rapidly changing lifestyle dynamics and product interests. Consider the reality that consumers are becoming more interested in a host of trends, including advanced technology, greener lifestyles, and saving money, as quickly as they appear on the scene. To be sure, distractions come not only from the state of the economy but also from numerous other sources.

Increased access to information is a rather large source of distraction for consumers today. Consumers are spending more and more time learning all the new ways that entertainment, education, or work can enhance their lives. They are learning from others, like their kids or coworkers. They log on to the Internet to learn about emerging forms of technology, to do background research before making a purchase, and to discover how to live in the new world of consumption. They are trying to figure out if it really pays to buy a lightbulb that promises to deliver seven years of use for four times the price of a traditional lightbulb. They are reading about new pricing strategies, borrowing money, and paying off debt. They are even saving for a change. Consumers are growing more diverse in their behavior and more in tune with the wider variety of options that has become a part of their everyday lives.

Just look at the increasing number of single mothers and fathers in the population. Parents who fall within this growing demographic need a different or expanded base of knowledge than do those who are married and are used to sharing or delegating certain decisions with their spouses. What's more, traditional parenting roles have changed, and as a result, consumers who at one point in time entrusted the purchasing process of a particular product to their spouses now are in charge of and/or more engaged in such purchases. Women today are taking over responsibilities that were once shared with or delegated to men, like wrestling with college applications and scholarships and saving up to fund their kids' college educations. Or how about purchasing the family car? In the past, this purchase was left in the hands of men. Today, however, women are tackling this formerly very gender-centric purchase and are buying as many cars as men. Women's increased purchasing power has shifted the consumer base of not just the automobile industry but retailers and manufacturers across the board, and those with traditionally male-centric purchasing processes and selling focuses have had to adjust accordingly.

Needless to say, thanks to the onslaught of information and purchasing options afforded them, consumers have become so distracted that they have entered so-called consumption comas. Waking consumers from out of their comas will require the full efforts of retailers and manufacturers. It won't just happen. Gone are the days when consumers purchased everything they wanted or even thought they remotely wanted. Consumers have established an actual decision-making process for their purchases and will be putting more thought into what they buy going forward.

Before you think about moving forward with your business, before you begin to market or even design your product, it is critical that you recognize the growing distractedness of your consumer base. It is up to you to proceed with the intention of waking your consumers from out of their comas.

CHAPTER 3

Change in Consumption

Consumers today are purchasing under duress. Regardless of whether they are mothers with children, single males, or fall within any other demographic, shoppers across the board are now forced to wrestle with every single purchase they make. Whereas impulse purchases were once the norm, consumers today have begun putting thought into all their purchasing decisions, which by consequence has inextricably altered their spending behavior.

The rules of consumer spending used to be: "I see it, I want it, I buy it, and I worry about how to pay for it later." Those rules have disappeared—at least for now. Consumers are no longer spending without regard for consequence. Instead, they are looking for ways to either stretch their dollars or to save for a rainy day.

The marketplace is beginning to see changes in consumers' consumption habits and abilities. Unlimited credit is a thing of the past, as are deals allowing consumers to buy now and stress out about credit payments later. All consumers, even those who are less than fiscally responsible, are beginning to learn the ins and outs of borrowing money. As a brief aside, I am amazed by the number of consumers I've interviewed who still have little to no knowledge of how credit cards work. They don't understand that when they pay off only the minimum balance due on their cards, they are not actually paying down their debt but rather are bearing the bare minimum cost of keeping their cards active. While my intention with this book is not to teach you how to manage your funds,

I am interested in helping you understand your consumers' spending behavior in the new economy. If you don't understand that the majority of your consumers are still relying on credit in an ever-tightening market to fund their purchases of your products, how will you possibly know if you're approaching them with a sales technique that is tailored to the way that they purchase?

The fact that consumers are purchasing under duress takes on additional significance when you consider the spending power of all those that are a part of the U.S. workforce, a figure that rounds out to approximately 100 million people. Multiply all those in the U.S. workforce by the amount of money that each employed person makes on average in one year, or about $50,000, and you can see that before taxes, the total U.S. workforce is worth roughly $500 billion in gross spending potential. Even after 20 percent of each person's gross income is subtracted from the equation to account for taxes, the U.S. workforce's net spending power still rounds out to around $400 billion. Next recognize that once consumers have paid their mortgages or rents, every penny of their $400 billion in spending power that remains is now governed by their newly incorporated tendencies to second-guess and overevaluate all of their purchases. Take consumers' cable bills, for example. While consumers might not question whether or not they can live without cable, they will be more inclined to find ways to cut down on the cost of their bill. They might consider altering their package options or bundling their cable with other new or preexisting services, like phone or Internet, in an effort to reduce their overall costs.

Because consumers are purchasing under duress, it is critical that you rethink how you are designing and marketing your products. An example: Consumers today want to buy multipurpose products. They want the equivalent of the Swiss army knife of products, an item that features so many functions that it becomes a necessity to their lifestyles. A blender is no longer expected to just blend. Now it has to be able to mix frozen drinks and chop food as well. Need another example? While refrigerators with built-in water filters might not be new enough to entice consumers to replace their older model appliances, those with TVs built in to the outside of the refrigerator door have a cutting-edge quality about them that persuades consumers to buy. All of this is to say that with each new product you develop, you need to be offering functions that surpass those of the traditional product.

It is important to understand the ways in which consumers' consumption habits are changing. Consumers are assessing their spending with greater scrutiny and are no longer buying products that offer anything less than the best value for the price. Sure, they still are willing at times to buy a singularly focused product—but only if that product can offer something that no other product can, like a distinguished brand or the best performance rating in class. What this means is that you will need to find a new trigger that will draw consumers' focus to your retail offerings or your product's message. You must develop products that will wow your consumers, things that will appeal to their sense of worth by serving as either short- or long-term money-saving investments. Just one look at recent NPD data on accessories reveals that consumers are placing an increasing amount of importance on purchasing investment-worthy items.

As Figure 3.1 shows, sales of men's watches are growing even though the rest of the market is in decline.

Not long ago, the trend among younger consumers was to gravitate away from singularly functional watches in favor of using multipurpose devices, like cell phones, as their timepieces of choice. As the sales upswing in Figure 3.1 indicates, however, even though they serve only one functional purpose, watches recently have been gaining popularity among men for their investment value. Male consumers have returned their loyalty to this product because they feel it will enhance their image, keep them punctual, and most importantly hold its value to some degree. As the watch example

Dollar Sales % Change

	08 vs. 07	Q4 '08 vs. Q4 '07
Total Accessories	-14.1%	-26.0%
Total Watches	8.8%	6.2%
Total Men	10.5%	20.8%
Total Women	6.3%	-13.5%

Source: NPD/Consumer Tracking Service

Figure 3.1 Investment Worthy Consumption

illustrates, consumers today are weathering the current economic storm by looking for products whose value withstands the test of time. And when they find such a product? Well, they have no problem changing the rules of their purchasing behavior to make room for it.

To be sure, as evidenced by the example of rising watch sales, consumers have drastically altered their spending behavior in response to the inclement economic conditions of late. After all, they are facing down a recession that is deeper and unlike any other they have seen in the recent past. But the bubble that brought about the recession of 2008–2009 had to burst. The U.S. economy could not have perpetually sustained its steep and protracted upward climb. Although it had become the norm for all cylinders of the U.S. economy to continually operate at full speed and steadily gain momentum, this new "normal" was anything but. Economies must ebb and flow. It is only natural, therefore, that the unrelenting growth in the job, real estate, and retail markets eventually exerted so much pressure on all facets of the U.S. economy that the entire financial system finally began spiraling downward. The decline had to come.

Yes, the bubble had to burst to preserve the long-term health of the U.S. economy, but rapid and simultaneous declines in a number of economic facets are not without their residual problems.

As evidenced by the current recession, the simultaneous declines in the housing market and the credit market, both at the consumer and retailer levels, have created a compression in the U.S. economy. I refer to this simultaneous squeeze in housing, credit, and pricing, all of which act together to put the squeeze on the consumer, as the Great Compression.

Let's look at the example of increasing gas prices once again as a means of explanation. As the price of gas rises, consumers begin to feel a strain on their overall financial situations. They hear and see news of fluctuating crude prices and wonder what effect these vacillations will have on the price of the gas they soon will be pumping into their cars. Eventually consumers begin to equate elevated prices at the pump with the weakening of the economy, and the task of filling up their gas tanks becomes a weekly (if not more frequent) and emotionally charged reminder of the instability of the economic situation in the United States. In the past, to mitigate their emotional reaction to rising prices at the pump, consumers had cut back on their driving and gas purchases—but only temporarily. Eventually, usually after about two months, they reverted back to their normal gas purchasing behavior. But an altogether new phenomenon is occurring during the current Great Compression. Even though prices at the pump are lower today than they were one year ago, consumers are maintaining their gas purchasing cutbacks (see Figure 3.2).

The oil industry is not the only sector that is experiencing declining revenues as a result of the Great Compression. Just look at average sales revenues within the retail sector. Stores are continually clearance-racking their merchandise and offering their customers steeper and steeper product discounts. These ongoing deals, coupled with special promotions like "buy one item, get the second one free," are resulting in seriously compressed retail revenues.

When I look at this situation from the business side of the equation, I find it interesting that stores are continuing to offer such

Gasoline Dollars Spent Trend (Billions)

460.3

362.6   382.8

370.0

27.3% $ Increase	5.6% $ Increase	20.2% $ Increase	19.6% $ Decrease
$78 Billion Dollar Increase	$20 Billion Dollar Increase	$77 Billion Dollar Increase	$90 Billion Dollar Decrease

JUN 06*   JUN 07*   JUN 08*   JUN 09*

Change in gallons purchased:

0.3%	1.9%	−0.2%	−2.5%

Figure 3.2 Falling demand and lower prices lead to a big drop in gasoline spending.

deep discounts to their consumers, even when their inventory levels are in line. But as it turns out, retailers have found that compressed consumers still feel as though they—and their bank accounts—are in need of such substantial markdowns. They have become used to these bargains, have come to expect them, and are motivated to purchase because of them. Eventually, however, retailers will have to put consumers through a strict regimen of what I call "Discount Detox" in order to help them feel comfortable purchasing full-priced products again.

Before businesses can properly detoxify consumers from their discount dependency, they will need to understand how buyers became reliant on store promotions in the first place. Every year for the previous five years from the time of this writing, I have seen stores accelerate the onset of the holiday retail season by invariably offering earlier and deeper discounts. And every year consumers respond to these discounts and begin their holiday shopping earlier than they did the year before in an effort to find better and better bargains. So, yes, these promotions work. But they work almost too well.

In many cases, these discounts have grown so aggressive and so pervasive that consumers have begun to expect them. In fact, many consumers are quite content to put off their holiday shopping until discount season begins. And they don't even need to delay their shopping much. Not long ago, Thanksgiving Day marked the onset of the prime holiday shopping season. But beginning in about 2006, retailers began discounting their merchandise even before Thanksgiving in an effort to lure sluggish holiday shoppers into their stores. And not only are sluggish shoppers rewarded during holiday shopping season, they now are continually granted everyday discounts. As a result, they have come to expect endless promotions, storewide sales, white sales, you name it, all the time and everywhere. If they aren't offered a discounted price on an item they want to purchase, they simply will go somewhere else to shop or they may not even shop at all.

The nonstop discounting of store merchandise is bound to obstruct the recovery of the retail sector. So the question is: how exactly do we wean consumers from these discounts? Subjecting them to Discount Detox will not be an easy task, especially considering the fact that retailers rely on product markdowns to entice customers—who generally prefer to shop only for what they want, when they want it—to purchase an item before they need it.

In the more than 30 years I have worked in the retail sector, I have never seen consumers show as much interest in buying seasonal merchandise when it's in season as they do now. Currently, my favorite example of seasonal merchandise that is almost never carried by stores when it is actually in season is swimwear. Good luck finding a swimsuit at a major department store during the summer, when you need it most. If you do manage to find a suit, odds are that it made its debut on the sales floor back in January or February, and it might even be the last remaining piece of swimwear in stock in the entire store. What's more, the likelihood that the swimsuit is both in style and fits you is pretty slim. But if you decide to go shopping during the summer for a swimsuit at a mass merchant like Wal-Mart or Target, you most likely will be overwhelmed by the array of options available to you. These retailers seem to have learned that there is a huge opportunity in simply giving consumers what they want, when they want it.

In my ongoing field research, I log the dates when various retailers set up their seasonal departments, as well as when each breaks them down. What I have found is that the vast majority of retailers, over 83 percent of those that I observe across the United States, completely misjudges the timing of consumers' desire for seasonal merchandise. To be fair, some retailers have begun to recognize the sales potential of seasonal merchandise and have slightly improved their approach to this sales category by offering their customers "transitional" seasonal merchandise. But while these retailers are taking a step in the right direction by giving their consumers what they want, when they want it, these efforts alone will not break consumers of their dependence on discounts. If retail and manufacturing brands really want to connect better with their consumers, they must first correctly identify and understand their customers' needs. Timing is everything in life, and it is even more so in retail. My experience in the retail industry has proven that if you make a product available, the consumer will find it and buy it. For example, when I was working as the president of WilliWear, I learned how to entice consumers to purchase the company's apparel year-round, instead of only in the springtime. While customers were enthusiastic about purchasing WilliWear's apparel in the spring, because of the considerably lightweight, Indian-grown cotton with which the clothing was made, they were reluctant to do so during the fall and winter, when the weather in many parts of the world calls for heavier fabrics. So to meet customers' fall and winter clothing needs, WilliWear simply began making apparel from heavier-weight cotton fabrics. As it turned out, the new heavier-weight collection ended up taking off like wildfire. WilliWear even earned the distinction of becoming one of the most successful clothing brands in the fashion industry the year the company introduced its lineup of heavier-weight cotton apparel.

When I look back now to that time, I can see that WilliWear became an incredible fashion success story because we were able to deliver what the customers wanted, when they wanted it. Never again would customers have to wait for the seasons to change before they could wear WilliWear clothing again because of yarn type, weight, or even color of the fabric it was made from. Remember the old rule that you should never wear white before Memorial Day? That rule has gone out the window. And with it has gone the consumer's inclination to wear cotton only in the spring and summer.

The key takeaway from the success that WilliWear enjoyed when it began offering heavier-weight cotton apparel year-round, in textures, weights, and colors that were more suited to fall season wardrobes, is that if you listen to your customers' needs, they will want your products. In today's challenging economy, consumers don't have the extra cash on hand to squirrel up and store products for future use. But if you offer your customers products they can use when they need to use them, they *will* buy them. And they won't even need to be lured into doing so with some kind of discount, deal, or store promotion. The sooner you learn that consumers buy based on their needs and begin to adjust your sales approach accordingly, the sooner you will be able to start cleansing them of their reliance on discounts.

Let's look at a few case studies of companies that have successfully detoxified consumers from their dependence on discounts, starting with Abercrombie & Fitch, the popular teen and young adult clothing retailer. Abercrombie is one of a handful of retailers that believes that not only does discounting lower company revenues and profits, it also jeopardizes the image of the brand. So to buck the trend of discounting that has been plaguing retailers across the board, Abercrombie only offers discounts on its clearance merchandise. Not one for fancy buy-one-get-one-free deals, super sales, or one-day-only discounts, Abercrombie has spent the last decade selling as much of its merchandise as possible at full price, marking down older items only when they are ready to be moved to the backroom for a clearance sale. For Abercrombie, maintaining the image of its store brand is more important than offering gimmicky, reputation-tarnishing discounts in an effort to beat last year's sales figures.

Next, consider Nintendo's approach to Discount Detox. In lieu of offering consumers package discounts or additional free games with their purchase of the Nintendo Wii gaming console, Nintendo decided to employ a tried-and-true sales technique to increase consumer demand. As almost any parent of an adolescent has discovered during the past three holiday seasons, finding a store that carries the Wii during the months of November and December has been a nearly impossible feat. In their frenzy to track down a Wii, some consumers even desperately started turning to online resale sites like eBay, where they would purchase the gaming consoles at higher prices than their retail value just so Junior wouldn't be disappointed come holiday time.

In my opinion, it's no coincidence that the Wii has been sold out in almost every store come crunch time in the holiday shopping season. In fact, I think it's a tactical move for Nintendo, which appears to be using none other than the old reliable sales method of supply and demand to push purchases of the Wii. By limiting the number of Wiis—or, in the case of Holiday 2008, Wii Fits (an exercise-focused video game bundle)—that it releases into the marketplace, Nintendo creates the perception that consumer demand for the gaming console is even higher than it actually is. This in turn only ups the ante, making finding and purchasing a Wii that much more essential to consumers. And what happens to consumers when they finally get their hands on a Wii? Their sense of accomplishment and satisfaction has never been higher.

It seems silly that a company would limit the amount of products it supplies to stores when it knows full well that the demand for that product will be high. It seems even sillier for a company to do so during such a critical selling time as the holiday season. Why wouldn't Nintendo just do what almost every other manufacturer would for any other product and flood the stores with Wiis? But it can't be pure coincidence that Wiis have been nowhere to be found for three holidays in a row. Is it possible that Nintendo simply understands that if it limits the supply of Wiis in the marketplace during strategic times of year, it can keep the demand for the gaming console high, which in turn lessens the odds that stores will have excess inventory and begin discounting the product? I think so.

Although most retailers seem to have forgotten the selling power of the old strategy of supply and demand, Nintendo sure hasn't. In fact, Nintendo seems to thrive on keeping consumer demand for their products greater than the actual supply of said products in the marketplace. Nintendo's sales tactic ultimately has adjusted consumers' expectations of finding a Wii on sale—or even at a discount! Who can worry about finding a Wii on sale when consumers can't even find a Wii to buy at full price? And when consumers finally do walk into a store and by some magical occurrence find a Wii on the shelf, they fear that if they don't grab it then and there, Junior is going to think that Santa doesn't love him. Discount Detox success!

Companies like Nintendo and Abercrombie, which have successfully weaned their customers off discounts, are well prepared for doing business in the new economy, wherein retailers are judged more for their profitability than for the volume of their sales growth. If you want your company to join in the ranks of Nintendo and Abercrombie, it is critical that you too stop indulging your customers' desire for discounts and start noticing that the rules of retail are about to change. Is your company ready to take on the challenge of the New Retail Rules? You're about to find out!

CHAPTER | **4**

The New Retail Rules

For the past decade, companies have been seeking out growth both organically, by increasing their sales revenue and migrating into expanded product offerings, and inorganically, by merging with and acquiring other companies in order to expand their brand portfolio. The onset in 2009 of the new economic frontier, however, has proven disastrous for the latter of these two growth strategies. Before I go on, let me be clear: inorganic growth is by no means impossible. Indeed, some big companies have done an excellent job of managing their acquisitions, thanks to the leadership, independence, and good judgment they brought to the table when they began building their portfolio of brands. But such successes definitely seem to be anything but the norm these days.

Why is this, you ask? It's simple, really: many larger companies failed to take the time before buying boutique brands to gain any understanding of how these smaller businesses had differentiated themselves from their competition, developed their specific personalities, and connected with their customers. It only makes sense, then, that so many acquiring companies, upon finding themselves saddled with brands for which they have no real feel, have begun selling off these smaller businesses as soon as they become drains on profits.

The one expression I find myself returning to quite often during my CEO coaching meetings is: "Get the core right." I have witnessed so many companies become distracted from their core business in their zeal to extract growth from their acquisitions. Rather than fixing or focusing on their core brand, these conglomerates took their eye off the ball and started relying on their acquisitions to grow their business.

Consider again the case of the automakers. Instead of designing and selling the types of cars that drivers wanted, American automakers opted instead to abandon their core focus and acquire brands that could add volume to their sales but not profits to their bottom lines. Look at General Motors, for example. General Motors added Hummer to its portfolio in 1999 only to sell the brand off in 2009 after filing for bankruptcy protection. Infer what you will from General Motors' recent sale of the Hummer brand. Maybe the initial purchase of the brand was a good decision for GM, maybe it was a bad decision. But, how did buying Hummer help General Motors develop the sedan that consumers have been clamoring for, one that delivers better fuel efficiency and reliability? It didn't.

Perhaps the more important questions are these: Have you recognized that the market has changed? Do you suspect that the old rules of selling no longer apply? Are you ready to learn and then apply a new set of rules when you sell your products? If you answered "yes" to these three questions, then you're ready for the New Retail Rules, which I'll describe in more detail in the sections that follow. As the world has changed, so have the rules by which we operate, and it is in this spirit that I offer up to you the New Retail Rules, a set of guidelines that I believe will help you rethink and refine your product offerings until they match your consumers' needs.

NEW RETAIL RULE #1: LESS IS MORE

The financial crisis of 2008–2009 has taught the business world that companies are not successful because they are big; they are successful because they run their businesses better than anyone else. And while many businesses today still are attempting to achieve overall growth by acquiring smaller companies or ramping up the sheer volume of their sales, this trend is on its way out of style. Companies will begin to be judged not by their volume growth but rather by their profitability, and if brands and retailers can't find ways to make greater profits on less volume, they will perish. After all, size doesn't matter to today's consumers. They want what they want, when they want it, and where they want it. Only those businesses that can deliver on or cater to these consumer needs and desires will survive in the new economy.

NEW RETAIL RULE #2: CORE PRODUCT GROWTH

Consumers want the best of what a company has to offer. They're not looking for brands that offer zillions of products. No, what they want are brands that are the best in class, brands that promise them the best products money can buy—and then follow through on their word. If you want to expand your company's business, you can no longer merely rely on your customers' brand loyalty. Instead, you must identify your single best product and then find natural areas in which to expand that product range. I've said this once, and I'll say it again: you must stick to your brand's core focus.

NEW RETAIL RULE #3: MULTITIERED PRODUCT OFFERINGS

Consumers today are craving the psychological comfort they feel when they purchase products that have brand recognition. It won't always be easy to soothe consumers' buying butterflies, especially for companies that deliver aspirational products that consumers have to dig deep into their pockets to pay for. But if these high-end brands want to preserve their consumer base—and their bottom line—they will need to dip into the wells of their creativity and develop more affordable, fair-value product offerings that even the most jittery of consumers would be enticed to purchase. Think about offering your product in three different tiers, ranging from "good" to "better" to "best." Differentiating between the product levels could be as easy as relabeling or rebranding each respective tier, or it could be as difficult as designing the same product offering in three different quality grades. But whatever you decide to do, it is critical that you offer your consumers the brand and product experiences they are looking for.

Still stuck? Let's look to the auto industry for guidance. Now, you're no doubt thinking: haven't automakers shown us what *not* to do? Well, you've got me there. Nevertheless, some car companies—for example, Mercedes, BMW, and Audi—actually do very well when it comes to providing their consumers with multi-tiered product offerings. These automakers all offer different classes of products, all of which are characterized by different feature grades and driving experiences, and no matter what car consumers decide to purchase, they are comforted by the heritage of the brand into which they are buying.

When you tier your product offerings, you allow a wide range of consumers to enter into your brand experience. They can find a point of entry with a lower-level product and then migrate upward to a more expensive product offering as they grow with the brand. So few companies truly understand how to tier their brand. I can't count how many times I've seen companies dilute their products in an attempt to create lower-end offerings that appeal to downmarket consumers. And the sad thing is, when they remove the very features that make both their products and their brand unique in order to decrease the price of their offerings, these companies don't even realize that they're taking the brand experience right out of the purchasing equation!

Learn from these companies' mistakes. Never lose focus on what makes your brand unique. Find ways to savor it. Challenge your team to preserve the essence of your brand when they design, market, and sell varying versions of your uniqueness. Don't lose it. Evolve it.

NEW RETAIL RULE #4: SERVICE MEANS A WHOLE LOT MORE

While price remains the number one factor that consumers consider before making a purchase, as the economy begins to enter into a period of recovery, service will step in as the second most important element in the value equation of a product purchase. As a result, it will become increasingly more important for brands, retailers, and service companies to clearly articulate and intensify their focus on customer service.

Today's consumers are waiting to see which brands will step up and be there for them not only today but tomorrow, too. There are countless companies out there that can provide short-term solutions to consumers' spending needs, so how is your business going to set itself apart from the rest of the pack? Start by offering consumers what they want: the entire package. Give them the best value for their money, the backing of a dependable brand, and customer service they won't be able to find anywhere else. And don't just grandstand about how great your customer service is. Truly ramp it up. Service is, after all, the perfect place to exceed your consumers' expectations. Which brings me to my next point.

NEW RETAIL RULE #5: EXCEED EXPECTATIONS

Who's the first person you should turn to when your company is in need of a marketing boost? Your director of marketing? A fancy marketing consulting firm? Wrong and wrong. The single best marketing agents your company can have is . . . your customers—that is, if you can get them to open up their mouth and pass along word of what great products or customer service you offer. But before you'll be able to pry loose their jaws and get their lips flapping, you first will need to understand what it is that they want—and then you not only have to deliver on it, but you will have to do so in a way that exceeds their greatest expectations.

The great thing about New Retail Rule #5 is: It's actually not that difficult to exceed your consumers' expectations. Say your customer expects that a product she ordered from you will be delivered in two to three weeks. Do what you can to make sure it gets there in one to two weeks. Or how about that customer who purchased a battery-operated product from you? Tuck the appropriate number and size of batteries into your product's packaging. What if your consumer bought a product that requires installation? Throw in free installation with the cost of delivery. See? Simple. Think about the product your customers are buying and how they will use it. Really try to understand their purchasing process, and then walk step by step through that process in their shoes, so that you can understand it from their point of view. Now go one step further. If some unforeseen problem occurs with the purchase or delivery of the product, go one step further than your last step. Give them every reason to tell all their friends about how great your product is and, even better, how great the experience of buying it from you was.

Don't believe me? Just walk with me, in my shoes, for a moment. I think you'll begin to see what I mean.

I travel a great deal. In fact, for forty-five out of fifty-two weeks in a year, I travel. Those of us who travel a great deal *par avion* have learned to roll with the punches. Cancellations, delays, lost luggage, and long lines are all part of the package. But on one of my many trips, I had an experience that was so unlike anything I have ever encountered that I *have* to share it with you. Flash back with me, if you will, to a day that started out just like any other.

On this particular day, I arrive at New York City's John F. Kennedy International Airport and proceed to Delta's ticket kiosk to check in for my flight to St. Louis. As is sometimes the case, the check-in process at the kiosk fumbles along until the computer eventually informs me that it is having trouble locating my reservation. "Please see a ticket agent," the kiosk kindly informs me. Not a big deal, I think. This happens from time to time when I check in at these kiosks.

So off to the ticket counter I go to wait on Delta's priority line with my fellow frequent flyers. I wait and I wait. Finally I get a little more aggressive and wave to get a ticket agent's attention. I walk up to her counter and hand her the paper the kiosk has printed out for me, and she starts tapping on her computer keyboard. Tapping. And tapping. And still more tapping. How about some more tapping? Finally, she speaks, and what comes out of her mouth? What is the first word she utters to me since my arrival at her counter? "Hah!" That's right, "Hah!" which she then punctuates with more tapping and key punching and now head shaking. "Oh my..." are the next words she speaks, followed once again by rapid typing. There's still no information coming my way, and she's still typing.

With each clack of the ticket agent's keyboard, another second marches right on by, and I eventually look down to my watch only to realize that 40 minutes have passed since the moment I first touched the kiosk screen to check in for my flight. Finally, the ticket agent looks up from her computer and says, "This is not good. You'll have to go over to that phone bank there and pick up the phone. The person on the other end of the line will help you." By this point in time, after 40 minutes of useless customer service, I have become less than accepting that, as I perceive it, the ticket agent has brushed me off. I ask her where I can find someone to assist me in person. She doesn't even respond to my question and instead waves the next person on line up to the ticket counter.

The ticket agent's curt manner and refusal to assist me have pretty well destroyed all my expectations of her, so I politely ask to speak with a supervisor. She ignores me. I am dangerously close to missing both my flight and my subsequent appointment in St. Louis, and furthermore, I have reached my limit, so I take matters into my own hands. I approach yet another ticket agent and politely ask, "Is *anyone* working here? Anyone at all? Do any of you care that there are customers here?" Well, that, it seems, pushed them right over the line of *their* limit.

Four ticket agents at the counter jump all over me like I am a terrorist. And they call airport security—which, I should mention, is the first time they have actually acted swiftly all day. The security officer arrives two minutes later and stares me down with his hand on his pistol, prepared to draw at a moment's notice. I take a deep breath and ask him if he wants to know why I am so upset. He actually relaxes and listens to my problem. He even chuckles with me when he realizes that I had remained rather calm about the whole situation, especially considering the way the Delta ticket agents had treated me. Finally he surveys the ticket counter, observing as the ticket agents ignore other customers in the same way they had ignored me, and says, "Come with me." He leads me over to the keyboard-happy ticket agent who had "assisted" me previously and stands at the ticket counter with me until the agent finally informs me that my flight has been canceled. So, this was how Delta treated its customers? Ignoring them, not smiling at them, attempting to intimidate them with armed guards, and so on. *This* was Delta's idea of service? Not in my book.

Follow my train of thought back with me to the ticket counter, where I am trying to book a seat on another St. Louis–bound flight for the same day. Eventually I am able to track down an open seat, but there are complications. Not only will I have to fork over more money to get to my final destination, but I'll be departing on a different airline than I had expected—American Airlines this time—on a flight that is scheduled to take off out of LaGuardia, New York City's other major airport. What's more, I'll have to endure a taxi ride in rush-hour traffic in my hop from airport to airport. Nevertheless, I thank the security officer and the ticket agent for their assistance, and then I embark on the next grueling leg of my adventure. Oh, yes, there's more.

Now, here is where the story takes an interesting twist. Initially, I head out to the taxi stand with the intention of grabbing a cab and scooting over to LaGuardia, but the line is ridiculously long. So I decide to use a little trick I picked up in my many years of traveling and jump over to another terminal in the hopes of finding a taxi stand with a shorter line. As I'm *en route* to the next terminal, I find myself near John F. Kennedy International Airport's American Airlines ticket counter, and in an effort to save a little money . . . just maybe . . . I decide to stop and purchase my ticket then and there.

As I approach the ticket counter to wait on American Airlines' check-in line, a gentleman from the first-class ticket counter waves me over to him. How nice of him, I think. He isn't busy with other customers, so I ask him if he would be able to process my ticket for my flight out of LaGuardia with service to St. Louis. He looks up my flight information, and guess what? The kind gentleman informs me that my flight actually is scheduled to depart from John F. Kennedy International Airport, from the very terminal in which I currently am standing. How lucky am *I*? I think.

Because he had helped me escape near-disaster, I decide to share the story of my latest travel escapade with the ticket agent, and what do you know? He tells me what the Delta ticket agent couldn't or wouldn't: the reason my flight had been canceled. As it turns out, all M80 aircrafts had been grounded that very morning so they could undergo safety inspections. Then, he one-ups himself by upgrading me to a first-class ticket and asking that I consider flying American the next time I book a flight. Not only did the

American Airlines ticket agent restore my faith in humanity, but he *also* exceeded my expectations! And thanks to the ticket agent's fantastic customer service, I now seek out American Airlines for my traveling needs.

Strive to follow the example that American Airlines has set. Learn how to empower those members of your team that come into contact with your customers so that both they and your company can exceed expectations. Your employees not only need to be capable of solving problems but they also must be equipped to communicate with and extend options to your customers. If both you and your team understand the importance and value of simple courtesies like discounts, upgrades, or even overnight shipping, all of which can make your customers feel wanted and important, you'll be that much better off in the new economy. Don't just deliver on expectations. Exceed them.

NEW RETAIL RULE #6: DELIVER MESSAGES DIRECTLY TO CONSUMERS

The one big mistake that companies make more often than almost any other is allowing a third party to deliver their message.

If you think that you can simply sell your products to retailers and then sit back and relax as they exert the same amount of energy to promote your merchandise that you would, think again. Retailers care first and foremost about increasing store traffic, and their primary vehicle for doing so is offering the lowest prices around. So while you'd be quite pleased if they lavished your new high-end product with front-of-store placement or front-page circular callouts, retailers are more focused on advertising and hyping their best-prices-of-the-season promotion, their 40-to-50-percent-off sale, or their blowout bargain of the year. Retailers' selling and promotional tactics don't do a great job of communicating your product's message and capabilities to end consumers, do they? So, what's a brand to do? As I see the situation, you have three simple tasks ahead of you.

First, recognize that your product must be able to sing solo. If you have the option of displaying signage or your product's packaging in stores, you must do so in a way that directly conveys the benefits of your product to your consumers. Not enough brands effectively utilize their product's packaging. They blast their company logo across precious packaging space, leaving little—if any—space for the product's specifications, which usually are cramped down into fine print. Now, think about it: Why would potential customers buy your product if the only details on the packaging that specify its amazing features are written in such a small font that they can't even read them? Which leads me to my next point: make sure that consumers understand and can easily articulate the benefits of buying your products. Remember, consumers are your most powerful marketing tool, so arm them with the information they need to effectively communicate your message to others. And third, be the shepherd of your own advertisements. Don't rely on the advertisements of third parties to communicate with your consumers. Use your own. Uncover new ways to reach out not only to your core customers but also to potential growth markets. And when you do reach out to them, speak directly to them. If direct communication isn't your strong suit, look to the pharmaceutical industry for guidance. Pharmaceutical companies have been personally interacting with their consumers through direct advertisements for years now, and the sheer power of their campaigns is a sight to behold. Whereas pharmaceutical companies once just sat back and crossed their fingers in the hopes that doctors would treat patients with their products, now consumers walk into their doctor's appointments seeking a specific brand of medicine that they believe will alleviate their ailments. In essence, thanks to their direct-to-consumer advertisements, pharmaceutical companies have empowered consumers to become influential players in the prescription equation.

If you're unsure of which advertising avenue to pursue, consider marketing with social media, which has emerged as an increasingly effective way for companies to communicate directly with their consumers. Social media platforms allow for direct-to-consumer messaging at the same time that they give consumers the opportunity to directly interact with your brand. No matter the demographic to which your company markets itself, be it grade-school kids or baby boomers, there is no better way to reach your target audience than with this new form of communication. And keep the following in mind:

The amount of time that elapsed before 50 million people embraced:

- The radio – 38 years
- The television – 13 years
- The Internet – 4 years
- The iPod – 3 years
- Facebook – 2 years

The world is rapidly evolving, and the advent and widespread adoption of such social media platforms as Facebook, MySpace, LinkedIn, and Twitter demonstrate just how influential the power of direct communication has become. As quickly as these new media outlets are growing, their pace is not nearly as accelerated as that with which the old methods of communicating your product are fading into obsolescence. Don't let yourself fall behind.

NEW RETAIL RULE #7: MULTIPLE MARKETING MESSAGES

When I review companies' marketing plans, I often am amazed at how finely focused these businesses are on whom they perceive to be their primary buyers. But a company's marketing and messaging efforts need to reach beyond its core customer base. If your company isn't open to potential growth markets or even a new consumer demographic, you actually can do damage to your business—and your bottom line.

So, say your company sells anti-aging skin care products. While the majority of your sales efforts probably will be targeted to consumers who are over the age of 45, you can't lose sight of the fact that younger consumers are interested in preventing the aging process too. Don't be afraid to widen your focus, a little bit at a time. Just because you're in the anti-aging skin care business doesn't mean you always should be selling your products to the 45-and-up demographic. Consider eventually widening your scope to include consumers over the age of 35, and then maybe to teens and twentysomethings too. Keep in mind, however, that not all markets want to hear the same marketing message, nor will they be using the same media sources to access it. Your message will reach a wider audience if you look to adjust where and how you deliver it.

NEW RETAIL RULE #8: OFFER DISTINCTIVE PRODUCTS

In today's retail reality, consumers are presented with an endless amount of products to choose from, with more cropping up every day. How are you going to ensure that your product is unique or distinctive enough to stand out from the competition and grab your customer's eye?

Let's start out simply. If your company already offers a cache of distinctive products, alert consumers to this fact. And if your products aren't so different from anything else on the shelf? Find a way to get consumers to think of them as unique. Take a page from the playbook of retailers, which are getting into the game by creating their own brands or by slapping private labels on their own previously generic, store-brand items in an attempt to neutralize consumers' inclination to buy pure brands.

Just as retailers are raising their games by improving their product offerings and differentiating them from the competition, you must do the same. Don't fall behind these dynamic changes in the retail industry just because you think that your brand carries strong consumer awareness. Big-box stores will promote their store-brand products very aggressively, challenging name brands as we know them to even keep pace.

Consumers will purchase those products that exactly match their needs and desires, and if you're skeptical as to whether such products exist, I'll have to ask you to turn your attention to the utter masses of offerings in your local superstore's toothpaste aisle. Want toothpaste that whitens your teeth and tastes like orange? Check and check. Or how about one that strengthens your enamel, is sensitive on teeth, and tastes like cinnamon? Check, check, and check! Consumers have learned that no matter how many combinations of features they want in a product, they will be able to find one to their exact specifications. And when they do find a product that offers every feature they're looking for, they will become loyal to the brand that carries it. Maintain the core of your business, but don't be afraid to add to and evolve your product offerings. Build on your products' core essence and on the strength of their integrity.

CHAPTER | 5

The Seven Stages of Business

As soon as a business is born, it begins constantly progressing through the seven cyclical stages of operations-based activity. No matter which stage of this cycle of operations your business currently finds itself in, it gradually will move onward, coursing through each of the seven stages until it has come full circle (see Figure 5.1). As we move forward together, keep in mind that the

Figure 5.1 Seven Stages of a Business Cycle

process of cycling through the seven stages of business requires constant examination and evaluation. I encourage you to approach learning about the business cycle in the same manner.

STAGE 1: LOGISTICS

After a company has been established and has proven that its general principles are solid, its management team must begin evaluating the logistics of the business and determine how to better support its operations and growth opportunities. The following are key logistical systems and processes that management teams must examine, evaluate, and then update or upgrade as necessary:

- The backroom process
- The infrastructure
- The support processes
- IT (information technologies) systems

Just a few short years ago, retailers shifted the concentration of their focus onto updating their business logistics, a long-overdue strategic move that prompted manufacturers to begin evaluating their logistics as well. Even Wall Street got excited by the news that many publicly traded companies would be addressing the backroom costs of their business models in order to generate greater profits. Bankers would now be able to use the information gleaned from evaluations of companies' major systems or processes to determine if they were on the right track for growth and direct their investments accordingly.

STAGE 2: PRODUCTION

After a company has thoroughly evaluated the effectiveness of its logistics and operations, it next must turn a discerning eye to its product offerings. Companies need to constantly be asking them-selves, "Is this product right for our business? How can we take it to the next level and align it with our consumers' desires?" If they find that their products aren't satisfying customers' wants and needs, companies can either start over from scratch or update their existing inventory. In the end, no matter what companies decide to do to improve their product offerings, as long as they do it right, they will be able to become better connected with their customers.

Consider automakers' recent attempts to review their product offerings. Not too long ago, two conflicting trends bubbled into the automobile industry: giving automakers the choice to either ride the winds of one fad and build more powerful sports utility vehicles (SUVs) into the car lineups or select the opposing course and introduce cars with better fuel efficiency into their showrooms. General Motors' product evaluations led them to follow the first trend and invest in Hummer, whereas one of Mercedes Benz's subsidiary companies decided on the second trend and introduced the Smart Car to the American car market. Now, which of these automakers' new product offerings do you think made more sense? Did I mention that at the same time that these two divergent prod-uct paths emerged, gas prices were rising to all-time highs? That piece of information should help you out with the answer.

Or look at recent efforts undertaken by the fashion industry to expand or improve upon its product offerings. A few companies, in an attempt to make their products more relevant to a wider con-sumer base, decided to begin offering their apparel with more extensive sizing options. In a classic case of "keeping up with the Joneses," a whole score of fashion designers then jumped on the bandwagon and began selling in a new array of larger-sized cloth-ing to department stores. With so many brands offering so much apparel in the larger sizes that plus-sized consumers need, it didn't take long for the market to become glutted with plus-sized clothing. And it didn't help that fashion designers were so busy incorporating these additional apparel offerings into their repertoire that they forgot to inform plus-sized consumers that their clothing needs were being addressed.

Retailers reacted to the sudden increase in sizing options by placing more plus-sized products on the sales floor and moving them to a more valuable retail space, alongside the regular-sized merchandise, in an attempt to give the larger apparel a chance to flourish. But plus-sized consumers, long-ignored by the fashion industry, never really had a chance to show their enthusiasm for these new product offerings. Yes, retailers had made plus-sized clothing available to their consumers. They even gave it ideal retail space. But within months—literally months—it was taken off the sales floor. After one season, just three months, retailers didn't get the sales volume they wanted from plus-sized consumers, so they quickly abandoned this market and began expanding their regular-sized product offerings. In retail, the kind of prime store real estate that the plus-sized clothing had been granted requires instant results, and these new larger-sized apparel lines couldn't deliver on that mandate. The rate of sales in the plus-sized clothing market just wasn't up to speed with retailers' expectations, and when products can't produce, they must vamoose.

I recall being asked by one major retailer, "Why didn't plus-sized clothing work in our stores?" I told this individual that first and foremost, not all consumers change their behavior as quickly as he'd like them to. Then, I asked this person how he would feel if stores had ignored his needs for decades and then, all of a sudden, thought to say hello to him, yet didn't quite speak up loudly enough for him to actually *hear* that hello. "How would you know how to respond—or even that you *could* respond—to such muffled hellos?" I asked him. The message that I wanted to relay to this particular person was that not only did he forget to inform plus-sized consumers that clothing items catering to their needs were being carried in his stores, but he also had snubbed this demographic for years.

He needed to understand that even though his stores had neglected plus-sized consumers, those people still had needed clothes. They couldn't go naked, after all. So they had adapted. They had learned to shop elsewhere and less frequently than regular-sized consumers. After all, only a few stores stocked the products that they needed anyway. It would take time and patience for more mainstream retailers like his to eventually gain plus-sized consumers' interest, trust, and business, thanks to the years they had spent giving these shoppers the cold shoulder. What's more, it would take even more time for word of mouth of his new product offerings to circulate among the right crowds of people. Plus-sized clothing didn't work in his stores because he didn't even wait long enough to *see* if it would work. Instead, he quickly abandoned the idea, moving his focus away once again from larger-sized products.

So, the real moral of this story is: yes, if you build it, they will come—but you must be patient enough to give them the time they need to learn about what you have built. Consumers can change—and they can even do so rapidly—but they will never adjust their purchasing routines as quickly as you might want them to. Dramatic changes in consumption habits don't happen overnight, so learn to be patient.

The point here is that all industries and companies go through the product evaluation process, but not all of them make the right decisions when it comes to actually expanding or updating their product offerings. Do everything you can to ensure that when you do evaluate your products, you do so carefully, thoroughly, and with consumers' desires at the forefront of your mind, lest you risk destabilizing the balance of your company's objectives.

STAGE 3: MERCHANDISE

In the next stage of the business cycle, companies must determine how much and in what kinds of merchandise they should be investing.

Let's take our example of companies immersed in the merchandising stage of business from the 2008 holiday season, discussed in Chapter 3. In August 2008, retailers began assessing their inventory levels in order to estimate the extent of "on order" commitments they should place for the upcoming holiday season. Although the housing market had dropped significantly by late summer of 2008, retail still was humming along, so retailers decided that they needed to be only a little conservative with their holiday "on orders." They went ahead and aligned their orders with those they had placed in previous years, deciding not to reduce their inventory or commitment levels because, after all, even though the market was down, retails sales were doing just fine.

Come September, however, with the market still in decline, it had become evident to retailers that cutting back on their "on orders" would have been the more prudent course to take. Unfortunately, the damage already had been done, and stores' inventory levels were packed full of more merchandise than consumers needed or desired. Even though stores had evaluated their merchandise and taken stock of their inventory levels, they had failed to see that a perfect storm was brewing in the markets. By the time the holiday season rolled around, consumers had stopped spending, and no product in stores' inventories was exciting or new enough to convince them otherwise. With inventories chock-full of peak holiday-level amounts of merchandise, stores had no choice but to deeply discount their wares in the hopes of driving sales. Their discounts were so steep that retailers were practically paying consumers to shop in their stores.

During that 2008 holiday season, stores were offering their merchandise at discounts of up to 75 percent off, and then were giving their consumers an additional 25 percent off on top of that. Because stores had discounted their items by 75 percent and then reduced prices again by an additional 25 percent, some consumers thought that they could purchase this merchandise at 100 percent off—or free of charge. In reality, this wasn't the case. While the retail environment was bad, it wasn't so bad that stores were *giving* their products away! But they were selling their merchandise, regardless of how new or high end it was, at the lowest prices consumers had ever seen in their lifetimes. Even the traditional year-end clearance sales of the past couldn't hold a candle to the kinds of promotions being offered by stores during the holiday season of 2008.

What quickly was becoming clear was that retailers were facing no ordinary economic environment. Even the catastrophic terrorist attacks on the World Trade Center and the subsequent terrorist threats on public places—and specifically malls—in 2001 weren't enough to negatively impact that year's holiday retail sales. But now the holiday season, which had always—almost invincibly—resulted in booming retail sales, suddenly had become vulnerable. It was unlike anything the retail market had ever seen before.

The holiday season of 2008 was so uniquely disastrous for a number of reasons. First, there were indications right from the onset of holiday 2008 that when economists looked back on that season's retail sales, "growth" would not be a word they would use to describe the situation. Second, while the holiday shopping season always offers up its fair share of rebates and sales, discounts became not just part of but rather *the entire story* in 2008. And the third reason that this holiday was so different from any other that had come before it is that retailers' failure to focus on how much and what kinds of merchandise they should be stocking gave way to their overwhelmingly concentrated focus on discounts.

This is not to say that it would have been easy for retailers to zero in on exactly how much and what kinds of products they should have put "on order" back in August 2008 for the forthcoming holiday season. After all, thanks to year after year of roaring holiday sales, even the industries that were supplying their merchandise to retailers had grown complacent and had put virtually no new products into the marketplace. The handful of products that had hit the market that year did do well—very well, actually—but there were so few new items that retailers couldn't possibly hope to use them to drive the brunt of their sales momentum. Because stores had forgotten the importance of the business cycle's merchandising stage, all that was left for them to do was lower prices and offer discounts. But it was too late in the holiday season for these tactics to have any real effect on retailers' bottom lines. Consumers already had lost interest, and their desire to shop and ultimately their inclination to buy continued to drop deeper and deeper. Merchandise had officially lost its way.

With the economy shrinking and stores' shelves stocked to the rafters with boring merchandise, holiday 2008 was a disaster waiting to happen. In fact, it was the worst holiday season for stores in over a decade, but despite the scale and magnitude of this shopping setback, unfortunately not enough retailers and manufacturers walked away from it with the right lesson in tow. The problem wasn't that consumers weren't willing to spend their money. Rather, it was that retailers and manufacturers had gotten lazy, had taken the merchandising phase of the business cycle for granted, and had introduced so few new products to the market that consumers would be excited about spending their money on. They had forgotten to invest in their own future.

I guess I shouldn't be all that surprised at what transpired in the retail market during holiday 2008. After all, in my frequent meetings with senior management professionals of major companies, I often see that they routinely have neglected to focus on the merchandising stage of the business cycle. Instead, companies opt to simply base the composition of their product portfolios on those items that historically have sold well in the marketplace. They often—too often—rely too heavily upon the successes of their flagship products, keeping these items in their mix of product offerings until the market or product shelf demands a change. And even then, when diversification is called for, businesses merely will make slight cosmetic adjustments or updates to their bellwether products. At the end of the day, making a few minor tweaks here and there to a preexisting product is far more cost effective than taking a risk and creating an altogether new offering whose shelf appeal might be hit or miss. But when businesses only continue to try to breathe new life into their older offerings, they are missing out on the opportunity to create the kinds of fresh and exciting products that will lure in consumers. Businesses need to mix in new merchandise with their repeat, heritage items if they want to strike a successful balance of offerings in their product portfolios.

If mixing up your merchandise isn't exactly your company's forte, perhaps you should take a look at Nabisco's efforts to diversify its Oreo cookie offerings. How could Nabisco tinker with the formula for one of the world's most popular products? Successfully! In fact, Nabisco has found numerous ways to capitalize on the heritage of their iconic Oreo cookie, resulting in everything from Double Stuf Oreos to Chocolate Fudge Mint Oreos to 100 Calorie Packs Oreos to their most recent Oreo Cakesters. And as of this book's publication, the success of Oreo Cakesters has led Nabisco to create even more new flavors within that product line alone.

Nabisco truly has achieved great balance in the merchandising stage of the business cycle not only by maintaining the success of the Oreo but also by innovating it, redefining it, and leveraging its core brand power to create altogether new Oreo products. Just think for a second: Nabisco didn't eliminate its core Oreo product like Coca-Cola did when it replaced its Classic Coca-Cola formula with New Coke, only to regroup and bring back the original product after great consumer uproar. No, Nabisco kept the original Oreo intact and then built upon its success by adding new colors, flavors, and sizes of the cookie to its product range. And then, once it determined which of its new products consumers were greeting with enthusiasm, Nabisco built upon the success of those cookies by introducing them in varying flavors, colors, and sizes. In doing so, Nabisco not only expanded upon its product portfolio, it also appealed itself to an ever-expanding consumer base. Nabisco evaluated itself and its product offerings during the merchandising phase of the business cycle and then built its brand off of its findings.

STAGE 4: STAFFING

After your business has made its way successfully through the merchandising stage by pinning down your product mix and aligning your logistics and production systems, your management team must turn its focus to the staffing stage of the business cycle. Do you have the right mix of people at your company? Do you have enough employees? Too many? Are all of your employees working in positions that are best suited for their skills and backgrounds? Are you continuing to add staff members as your business continues to grow? Are you evaluating the performance of each of your employees to ensure not only that their potential is being realized but also that they are contributing to the optimum operating efficiency of your business?

As businesses grow, all too often they are so focused on lining up their backroom costs and enhancing their product mixes that they neglect to consider the efficiency of their staff. They fail to see that from time to time a more senior employee can better meet the requirements of a particular job than two less senior employees tasked with the same responsibility can—or that perhaps the opposite is true. But the point is that you must take the time to *constantly* evaluate your staffing needs if you want your company to avoid falling into a staffing stagnation. These evaluations are critical during all of the stages of the business cycle and should be folded into the overriding culture of a company. It is only by continually reviewing, addressing, and assessing staffing needs and skill sets that companies will be able to maintain their efficiency and growth potential and stave off complacency, which is the worst trait that can infect your company.

Just look at the mountain of problems that arose when the automobile industry failed to pay due diligence to the staffing stage of the business cycle and grew complacent in its day-to-day operations. First their products began regressing until they no longer met consumer desires, and then their methods of marketing and selling their cars did too. Eventually their woes piled up so high that the entire house of cards came tumbling down, catapulting automakers from growth mode to survival mode. When most other companies are forced into survival mode, the first move they usually make is to begin laying off employees. The senior executives at American automobile manufacturers, however, had been running their staffs according to yesterday's standards and were forced to negotiate concessions into their unionized employees' contract agreements before any staffing changes could be made. The failure of automakers to regularly address and adjust their staffing needs led to the near collapse of a few major companies, the closure of several manufacturing plants across the United States, and economic fallout in the very cities that once sustained the automobile industry. Now, ask yourself: is complacency infectious? I think so.

Indeed, when it is ignored or left unaddressed, the staffing stage of the business cycle can have a seriously treacherous impact both on companies and their employees. And if the previous example of the automobile industry *still* doesn't convince you of this fact, just look at how many other companies and employees across a range of industries were blindsided by the current economic downturn. Because they were not paying close enough attention to their staffing needs, come financial crunch time, the first costs that companies shed were their employees' salaries. As a result, the unemployment rate has skyrocketed, and layoffs have become rampant in almost every sector imaginable. In fact, many companies have posted 4 to 5 percent layoff rates in the aftermath of the economic slowdown.

This unfortunate statistic doesn't necessarily trouble me, as I consider an elevated unemployment rate part of the natural ebb and flow of business and the overall economy. But what does concern me is that when the economic downturn forced them to assess their staffing needs, many companies found that not only were they bloated with employees but they were employing staff in all the wrong departments. Now, I'm not coldhearted. I know how terrible it is for someone to lose his or her job. But at the same time, businesses from time to time have no option but to shed staff. Sure, when a company is consistently growing, it can't fill open job positions fast enough. But at some point in time, business will start to decline, staff will need to be cut, and job roles will have to be adjusted. And in the end, the staffing changes brought on by the natural ebb of business always seem to fall into place, with truly valuable employees finding ways to do more work more quickly and tackle new responsibilities as they arise.

So to reiterate, businesses need to keep a steady eye on and regularly evaluate their staffing needs to ensure that the right people are in the right place, driving the engine of their business as efficiently as possible. Don't accept the status quo of your workforce. Find those employees who not only will expertly perform their current job functions but that also will repeatedly raise the bar for themselves and your company by finding new and innovative ways to improve your products. Go out and gather key players that will feed new ideas, efficiencies, and energy to your core business, and then, when you find these rare individuals, protect them, reward them, and secure them.

STAGE 5: REAL ESTATE

If you let your mind wander back to when the economic downturn of 2008–2009 was at its worst, you might remember passing by a strip mall or a crowded retail center in your hometown only to discover that your favorite fast-food chain or coffee franchise had closed its doors. Although it might have been inconvenient for you that one of your local eateries had gone out of business, these restaurant closings were almost certainly not due to happenstance. More likely, they were probably the result of calculated decisions made during the real estate stage of the business cycle, during which companies actively evaluate the necessity of every store or remote office in their holdings. And while the economic downturn presumably was the underlying reason so many companies recently have become more attuned to this fifth stage of business, it is my hope that your company will be smart enough to voluntarily begin assessing how constructive your physical growth has been to your overall success.

Despite its importance to the cycle of business, the many-layered real estate stage is seldom addressed by companies in a timely manner. In fact, companies generally wait to ponder their real estate holdings until one of the following two scenarios arises: either their business is booming so much that they are bursting at the seams or they are bleeding profits so profusely that their only option is to sell off remote or secondary locations in an attempt to save their bottom line. Given today's economic climate, companies more often than not are falling into the latter of these two camps, leading manufacturers, servicers, and even retailers to closely examine their every expense and determine the true worth of their real estate investments.

To be sure, as of this book's publication, the dust has begun to clear around the disastrous recession of 2008–2009. The major news outlets now are reporting that the economy has begun to stabilize, and the road to financial recovery appears to be close at hand. But don't be surprised if you tune into your local news station in the near future only to hear a report on the record numbers of store closings in your hometown or the vast amounts of vacant commercial real estate holdings in your city's retail district. Or perhaps you'll flip the channel to an investigative news report on what happens when abandoned big-box stores and car dealerships are left to sit as idle and empty reminders of "the way things were."

You see, when it comes to commercial real estate, a funny thing happens over the course of an economic downturn. Even when the economy begins to show signs of life, many companies still are stuck in the throes of the real estate stage, waiting out the often lengthy process of terminating their leases or closing on the sales of their commercial properties before they can continue riding through the business cycle. As a result, commercial real estate generally is the last sector to be affected by an economic slowdown and, as logically follows, the last one to recover. If you constantly review and assess your real estate holdings, however, paring away those real estate properties that are of lesser value while holding on to those whose profitability is obvious, your company will be able to move fluidly through the real estate stage and continue on to the next stage of business.

STAGE 6: REBOUND

After you have strategically maneuvered your way through the real estate stage of the business cycle, weeding out unnecessary or profit-draining properties and drawing in income from the sales of those holdings, your company will begin to see signs of stabilization springing to the surface of its daily business. At this point in time, you will have entered the rebound stage of business, a period during which your company must focus its energy on moving forward and begin taking advantage of the real opportunities that are presented to it. If your company has managed to reach the rebound stage of the business life cycle, it finally will be poised for growth once again. But be careful: it is just as tricky to correctly read stabilization as it is easy to fall prey to a false rebound. My research has shown that even if you have posted one or two months of increased consumer spending and confidence following an economic or company downturn, such trends generally are not true indicators of stabilization. More often, I find that it takes at least three to four months for the real signs of stability to appear.

Because I was wary of being duped by what I perceived to be early signs of stabilization, when the NPD Consumer Spending Indicator predicted in January 2009 that economic stabilization had arrived, I was not so ready to make the same call just yet. February rolled around, and consumer sentiment held, suggesting that they perhaps were even weathering the storm of job losses that had occurred that month, but I still was not convinced that the economy was entering a period of stabilization. But then, when consumers held steady in March for the third month in a row, I had my clear signal that stability was indeed settling in.

Yes, the economy was far from flawless. In fact, whereas conventionally it is companies that first begin to recuperate from extended time periods of financial shellshock, it was consumers who were leading the recovery charge in March 2009. But in the end, it didn't matter who was steering whom toward recovery. It didn't matter that businesses were going to wait until consumers were spending regularly again before they opened up their gates to investments. By this point of time in the recession, consumers and companies alike already had discovered that their new economic reality was governed by an entirely different set of rules than had ever before applied. All that mattered in the end was that, finally, and ever so steadily, the economy had started to turn around.

So, yes, everything has begun working itself out. At the time of this book's publication, the economy is even posting signs of growth, and many companies—and even some banks—are beginning to prosper once again. When all is said and done, however, when we're 10 or 20 years past the recession of 2008–2009, economists no doubt will look back at this time in economic history and see that the smartest companies were those that refused to merely stand still and wait around for the first signs of economic turnaround before forging ahead. As I frequently tell my clients: *"Just take the first step!"* Resist the urge to sit tight until the economy indicates to you that it's time to start thinking about your company's growth. Don't let yourself sink into the quicksand while your competition prepares itself to emerge from the poor economic conditions better, faster, and stronger than you. Instead, jump into the driver's seat and make growth happen. Be at the ready with a game plan, a product plan, and staffing plan. And be prepared to live, breathe, and perhaps most importantly communicate just how ready you are.

STAGE 7: GROWTH

It's undeniable: growth is great. Companies love it. They feel good about it. They embrace it. Yes, even though growth often means more work, more changes, and entirely new sets of rules, companies *love* growth. But, as it turns out, the kind of meteoric growth that had become the norm for so many companies in the years leading up to the 2008–2009 recession has ceased to exist—at least for now. Gone are the days when multiple industries would post growth rates in the double digits. Gone too are the days when businesses would open up multiple retail locations within five city blocks of one another. And while you might think that the new economic era that is upon us, characterized as it is by an absence of extreme growth, is anything but promising, I beg to differ.

I think it actually is beneficial that the world most likely will not witness the out-of-control growth that so characterized the post-dot-com economic boom at any time in the foreseeable future. After all, it is only with hindsight and distance from the post-dot-com economic boom that companies will begin to understand how, exactly, explosive growth led to the steep and destructive decline that brought about the recession of 2008–2009. So consider the indeterminate stretch of time between the moment you read this book and the next fiery period of economic growth as a gift—and use it wisely. Make the most of it by learning how to adequately manage and control the growth of your company. Sit with your thoughts until you come to the realization that blustering inorganic growth is no substitute for steady, disciplined organic growth.

Along those same lines, don't make the same mistakes in the future that so many other companies recently made when they tried to grow only through volume or acquisition. Volume growth all too often acts as a smoke screen, masking the cracks in the core foundation of a business. Instead, make the core of your business your first priority. Sure, you still can acquire a brand here or a company there whose product, message, and personality nicely meshes with your own. But first and foremost, focus on your core. Build on it. If you do so, regardless of whether your core is a tangible product or a particular service that your company provides, you quickly will be able to identify any fissures that form in your foundation and fill them before they bring your business tumbling to the ground.

Despite my words of warning, I have had the opportunity to work with many large companies that were so tempted by their perceived need to grow through acquisition that doing so became an addiction for them. One particular example of acquisition addiction that comes to mind occurred when four to five major manufacturers within the fashion industry got into the habit of buying out midsized companies. Some of the big folks were able to turn the midsized companies into commercial successes, but not before ripping their acquisitions' hearts and souls right out of them. Sure, these boutique brands were now volume drivers that could contribute to the major manufacturers' bottom lines, but they were also mere shells of their former, once-unique selves. And as we all know by now, when a company is stripped of its core, it can't help but flounder and sink. You shouldn't need more than one chance to guess what happened to most of the acquired midsized fashion companies. But on the bright side, one or two of the big folks were actually quite adept at managing the acquisitions process. These major manufacturers discovered that if they left the DNA of their acquired companies intact, their new brands would flourish—a little trick I like to call the "art of acquisitions." They chose slow, purposeful, calculated growth over growth for growth's sake. And most importantly? You guessed it: they didn't abandon the core.

! ! !

So, here we are, having worked our way through one full business cycle. If your company has been operational for a while, you probably recognized the seven stages of business as I walked you through them step by step. If you are relatively new to the business world, have confidence that once your company survives the cycle of business once, it will be able to forge ahead through the seven stages again and again. And if your business was able to weather the storm of the 2008–2009 recession, which took so many industries as its victims, take heart in the fact that you may never in your lifetime be forced to take on an economic downturn as severe as the one from which you've just emerged. After all, most recessions normally do not impact as many facets of the economy as that of 2008–2009 did. They usually don't result in bank failures, nor is it common for them to send shockwaves throughout the entire financial system. They rarely topple the housing market or eat away major portions of consumer and corporate wealth, and they seldom jolt the stock market up and down so quickly, so ferociously.

But if I'm wrong, if you somehow do find yourself face to face with the worst financial crisis the world has ever seen, the best advice I can give you is to stay on the course for growth. Properly evaluate your business, and do so in the same order that I've laid out for you in the preceding pages. Don't overreact, but don't underrespond either. Constantly consider all the ways your company could potentially fall prey to financial disaster, and then map out a plan of action for each scenario. And please don't stop seeking innovation and improvement. Find ways to be more efficient, and then find ways to motivate your employees to add even more efficiency to your company. Encourage your team members to turn their attention to your company's core focus. Be prepared to make midcourse corrections. Measure your current progress as well as your future needs. Don't sit still. Don't get stuck in the quicksand of fearing what's to come. Make a move, and if it happens to be the wrong one, simply take steps to correct your course. Be nimble, and by all means, be proactive. Take advantage of opportunities as they present themselves, lest your competition grab them up and pass you by.

I recently opened a fortune cookie that read: "Opportunities multiply as they are seized. They die when neglected." Most appropriate, I'd say.

PART 2

THE NEW CONSUMER

CHAPTER 6

New Committed Consumer

We all make changes to our personal habits on a yearly, monthly, or even daily basis in order to adapt to the various new realities that confront us over the course of our lives. Just-graduated high school seniors that once were able to rely on their parents to wake them up every morning for school adjust their behavior upon entering college and begin setting and waking themselves up to an alarm. Young couples that once were free to sleep through the night without interruption modify their sleeping behavior the moment they become parents to account for their newborn's needs and wants. The list of behavioral modifications that we almost subconsciously apply to our lives could go on and on. But I'd like to draw your attention to one area in particular where we constantly are tweaking, refining, and readjusting our behavior so that it aligns with the requirements of our lives: consumption.

How consumers spend depends entirely on what their lives demand of them. Here's what I mean: Have you ever known a young childless couple and then later watched them transition into their new lives as parents after having a baby? Did you notice how their spending priorities shifted from their own needs to their child's needs? Faced with the task of caring and providing for the new addition to their family, the new parents could no longer be financially accountable for only themselves, and so they changed their consumption habits accordingly. And consumers don't just adjust their spending behavior when doing so is an utter necessity, like in the foregoing example. When consumers agree to spend $300 on a pair of designer jeans even though five years ago they would have scoffed at such an inflated price, they are demonstrating a shift in their consumption habits. When consumers lose their BlackBerrys on the train and insist that they cannot go back to using standard cell phones, they are demonstrating a shift in their consumption habits. When consumers decide to take out a store credit card to fund a luxury purchase, they are demonstrating a shift in their consumption habits. You get my point: consumption is an evolutionary process that is driven by consumers as they constantly reevaluate, reassess, and revise their spending behavior. And if yours is a company that caters to consumers, it's up to you to keep up with their rate of change.

So, what's a business to do? It's easy enough to recognize that the retail environment is transitioning out of a period during which consumers were content to slap their money down on impulse buys and blithely sign their name along the dotted line on their credit card receipts without even a second thought. Indeed, as your bottom line probably has revealed to you, consumers are now consciously analyzing their every purchase and financial commitment and are choosing to spend less. But how to determine in today's seriously diminished economy why consumers *are* willing to part with the money that they are spending? With so many consumer dollars circulating around the marketplace, how can companies pinpoint the way that each bill has been spent? How can businesses possibly determine the primary motivation behind each consumer purchase? True, it may seem monumentally difficult to measure the precise degree to which consumers have revamped their buying habits. But if you break the consumption conundrum down to a microcosmic level and consider the purchases that eat up just one consumer's pay-check, if you were to comb over that person's preexisting bills while keeping a careful eye on what services and products he or she has agreed to pay for, you just might find what you're look-ing for. So, in the spirit of gaining a better understanding of con-sumer behavior, let's do just that.

! ! !

Our theoretical consumer has just received his biweekly pay-check, and he has decided to set a large amount of it aside to pay for the bills that he knows will be arriving later on in the month. First, he allots a good portion of his earnings to a jumble of recurring individualized expenses that he cannot really avoid, including mortgage or rent payments, car pay-ments, health-care costs, transportation costs, insurance, and, yes, food. He also remembers that payments are due for the compulsory lifestyle products that he decided to buy with installment agreements, such as the furniture and electronics he purchased with no-interest-first-year payment plans and the household appliances he acquired with zero percent financing. And while he's at it, he figures he might as well pay down a bit of the hefty amount of debt he has accumulated on his various credit cards. Then our theoretical consumer puts even more money aside to cover the costs he incurs from the long list of discretionary incidentals he has committed to, like his gym membership, his high-speed Internet service, and those monthly shipments of vitamin supplements he bought after viewing a late-night infomercial.

Take a look at the following list of incidentals that our theoretical consumer has purchased on either a subscription or monthly-fee basis. As you can see, the payment-plan products and services he is beholden to are probably very similar to your own:

Preexisting Consumption:

Gym	$25.00
Movie rentals	$9.99
Digital music	$9.99
Vitamins	$9.99
Cable	$59.99
High-speed Internet	$39.99
Cell phone	$59.00
Land-line phone	$29.00

New Consumption Commitments:

Social media accounts
Packages that bundle cable, telephone, and Internet services
Digital music subscriptions
Skin care regimen product programs
Movie rental programs (e.g., Netflix)

"Phew!" our theoretical consumer thinks. "I'm done with the bills for this month!" But not so fast. Ever since the recession of 2008–2009 began choking the economy—and consumers' pocketbooks—our theoretical consumer has been delaying the process of trudging into his local retailer and footing the bill for a few necessary replacement products and home appliances. As luck would have it, his washing machine *and* his microwave oven break down completely on the same day, escalating the importance of purchasing replacement items from "must do so sooner or later" to "must do so now." And though he certainly isn't happy that he is being forced into purchasing replacement products simply because his appliances decided to stop functioning, he has no choice but to dig even more deeply into his already greatly diminished discretionary income to afford these unplanned purchases. Fortunately, after he covers the costs of these replacement items, our theoretical consumer has successfully paid off his bills for the month. All that's left for him to do now is to sit back, hope that no new unforeseen expenses crop up, and wait for his next paycheck.

! ! !

So, now you have had a glimpse of all the cash that our theoretical consumer has committed to recurring expenses, ranging from rent to hot water to credit card payments. You've also added in his incidentals from the preceding list, noting that while each of these items individually puts only a small dent in his bank account, when they all are added up, their collective cost cuts a huge chunk out of the discretionary money he might otherwise spend on impulse purchases or replacement products. And then, just when you thought our theoretical consumer's wallet couldn't be stretched any further, a few unforeseen but necessary purchases reared up, taking with them all the discretionary dollars that he was holding in reserve.

As you clearly can see, our theoretical consumer's discretionary income has been slashed to the bare minimum. But wouldn't you agree, after taking stock of the kinds of items that he has purchased—as well as the way that he has financed them—that an interesting trend in consumer spending behavior is emerging here? Our theoretical consumer has dedicated so much of his income to covering the costs of commitment products that by the time he is presented with an opportunity to splurge on an impulse buy, he simply pauses to think for a moment, remembers how overleveraged and burdened by financial responsibility he already is, counts up how little discretionary cash he has on hand, and then says, "Thanks, but no, thanks." And if we truly believe our theoretical consumer's spending behavior is a microcosm for the wider consuming public, then it logically follows that consumers today are less tempted by impulse buys than they are by long-term commitment purchases.

Now, you're no doubt thinking: "Okay, I get it: Consumers are being more careful with their spending. They're no longer impulse shopping. They're more comfortable committing to a purchase plan. So, what's your point?" Why, thank you for asking. Yes, you probably understand by now that because consumers are spending so much of their income on preexisting financial obligations and unexpected purchases, they have far less money to spend on discretionary items and impulse buys. But do you know exactly how you're going to respond to this dramatic shift in consumer behavior? Have you considered how you are going to target consumers who are more strategic with their spending than they are impulsive and who would rather commit to long-term purchase plans than pay cash upfront? Do your company's marketing efforts emphasize that your products and payment plans will give your consumers the best bang for their buck? And have you explained to your consumers why committing to your products today will be more beneficial to them in the long run than it would be if they waited to purchase these items at a later date?

Today's commitment consumers are so financially shell-shocked that they're going to need more than a little prodding to make a purchase, so how are you going to grab their attention? Perhaps the tagline from the old Fram commercial for oil filters will serve as a useful guide for you. "You can pay me now . . . or you can pay me later," an automobile mechanic gently admonishes viewers, thinly implying that if they spend a little bit of money on car maintenance now, they might be able to save an enormous amount of money on replacing their entire carburetor or engine block later on. Of course, the specific style of marketing that Fram employed to sell oil filters back in 1971, when its commercial first aired, might not meet the needs of your company's message or products today. But you should at least consider taking a page from Fram's marketing playbook. After all, companies these days are employing scads of marketing techniques across every type of popular medium, from print to radio and television to the Internet, all in an attempt to win commitment of consumers' dollars. And if you do not do the same? You might as well kiss your consumers goodbye.

Just think for a moment about how flooded television programming is at all hours of the day and night with infomercials for various consumer products, ranging from detergents that clean with the power of oxygen to fancy markers that remove scratches from your car to brownie pans specifically designed to create outside edges on all of your baked goods. Now think about what *type* of products generally are offered in these infomercials. While it is true that not all of these products are tailored to committed consumers, many of them are. Vitamins, weight-loss programs, and other similar products all are being sold to consumers with the stipulation that if they don't cancel their commitments by a set date each month, they automatically will be shipped additional product and charged accordingly. And infomercial-type advertisements are not confined to just television anymore. All manner of blogs and Internet search sites reserve space on their home pages to host advertisements for online universities, teeth-whitening strips, brand commercials, you name it. And of course, no Web search would be complete without seeing an ad or two for male "enhancement" products!

Companies conjure up all kinds of ways to trick consumers into signing up for their long-term commitment offerings. The tactic employed by one particular software company is by far my favorite.

This company offers consumers a free CD filled with any sort of computing lesson they might desire, like "How to Buy and Sell on eBay" or "How to Maximize the Power of Microsoft Excel." Now, I'm not going to comment on whether or not the free CD actually teaches you the skills the company claims it will. But what I will tell you is that the lure of free learning doesn't come without a price. After it has successfully baited you with a free CD, this software company begins sending you a new computer program every month—and then sends you a bill for the cost of the disc. But do you know what? At no point in time during the software company's infomercial were you told that by agreeing to receive a free CD, you also were permitting the company to send you a different CD every month for a $49.95 fee. You learn about the purchasing commitment you have made later, either when you read the fine print on your free CD or when you inexplicably begin receiving computer programs in the mail. If you want to cancel your subscription, the only way to do so is to contact the software company, where the representative will tell you that she'd be happy to cancel your subscription, just as soon as you pay for the computer programs that you have received in the mail to date.

The software company's sales tactic is not at all uncommon. For instance, I recall watching an infomercial for a similar purchasing program involving vitamins. The company selling the vitamins guaranteed viewers their effectiveness, and then sealed the deal by adding that for buyers' added convenience, their supply would be replenished automatically every month and their credit cards would be charged accordingly. Indeed, companies across every imaginable industry are taking elaborate measures to draw in a commitment by consumers, and their efforts are paying off. Consumers today are buying lawn care services, alarm systems, weight-loss programs, fitness memberships, and cell phone plans, all on a committed basis.

Isn't it time you tried to attract a commitment from in your business as well? After all, the old rules of retail have gone out with the tide. No longer are consumers pouring dollar after discretionary dollar of their incomes into retail. Even if they wanted to finance expensive, one-time retail buys and impulse purchases, how could they afford to do so? Consumers' newfound love of commitment purchases has tied up every conceivable dollar of their income. They have effectively eliminated their own spending power and in doing so have reshaped the face of traditional retail as the world once knew it.

Indeed, a new era of committed consumption is upon us, bringing with it the necessity of rethinking the purchasing equation. So, analyze your offerings, as well as how often you make them available to your consumers—and then strategize a way to deliver them on a more frequent basis. Convince consumers that they need your products. Position your goods so that they become integral to your consumers' lives. Make it easy for consumers to buy your products on a regular basis by automatically replenishing their stock at set time intervals. Make it a given that consumers will be using your products for an extended period of time. Make it effortless for them to access what you are selling. *And do all of this as soon as you possibly can.*

CHAPTER | 7

The Global Consumer

There is no question that the world has entered into an era of global consumption. Thanks to the power of the Internet, consumers are no longer forced to scour the shelves of their regional retailers to locate the unique merchandise they so desire. Indeed, an entire world of products is now onstage online, accessible at the touch of a fingertip, and savvy companies have expanded the scope of their marketing efforts in an attempt to target consumers in every conceivable location worldwide.

Retail, too, is becoming increasingly more globalized, although the benefits and drawbacks of this particular phenomenon are debatable. During the glory days of retail, a walk down Manhattan's Fifth Avenue would have been mesmerizing, to say the least. Back then, only the most exclusive of retailers held shop on that storied avenue. As average consumers passed by, they would gaze longingly into the sparkling entrances of these storefronts, whose window displays brandished pieces of designer apparel and jewelry that they almost certainly would never have enough money in their lifetimes to afford. But if you walk down that same stretch of pavement today, you'll discover an altogether different retail reality. The east and west sides of the street are now lined with the same types of volume-oriented stores that consumers can find any day at any mall in the world. The same commercial spaces that once were occupied by boutique shops that carried the kind of luxury items that defied the imagination are now the retail dwellings of jeans stores, brand stores, and midlevel retailers, all of whose offerings are so homogenized that any given tourist visiting the Fifth Avenue satellite of one of these retailers will be able to purchase the exact same products that she would find on the shelves of the chain location in her own hometown. So, now, not only can shoppers access an entire world of goods anywhere and at any time, regardless of their—or the product's—country of origin, given that so many stores are selling their products online, but if they so desired, consumers could hop a flight to any city worldwide and shop at the same retailers they are accustomed to patronizing at home. Perhaps the biggest difference between a product bought in Milan and another purchased in Los Angeles is the kind of power cord you need to run it!

Indeed, the retail-shopping environment has become entirely globalized, and consumers have adapted accordingly. They have grown to expect that the products they are purchasing most likely were not manufactured in their home country, let alone in the hemisphere of the world that they live on! They don't really care about where any given product was made, nor are they concerned about where an item's parent company is headquartered. In fact, consumers rank country of origin among the bottom five reasons for why they purchase the items they do. The only major exception to this rule arises when the product consumers are buying is food, thanks to location-based outbreaks of *E. coli* and mad-cow disease, but even those concerns tend to be short-lived. Because they have become so accustomed to shopping online, where they can purchase a vast array of goods from every corner of the earth, consumers are turning more often to online product testimonials as the barometers against which they weigh their purchasing decisions. And as it turns out, these product testimonials have proven incredibly influential in their purchasing equations. It is incredible to witness how instrumental great testimonials from other shoppers who have bought and tested out a given product are in potential consumers' purchasing decisions. When a consumer reads that a product he is considering purchasing really worked for someone else or changed one consumer's life or helped one reviewer lose 30 pounds in just three hours, he thinks, "Hey, if it worked for that person, it just might work for me!"

I'm sure you can call to mind someone, maybe a friend or an acquaintance—or perhaps even yourself—whose first inclination it is to hop online and scan through product testimonials from shoppers all over the globe when he is trying to decide whether or not to purchase a particular item. Or perhaps you know of a bargain hunter who will sit for hours after deciding to purchase a product, Googling it until she locates a store whose combined product and shipping costs are lower than anyone else's. It doesn't matter to her where, exactly, her purchase is being shipped from, as long as it arrives intact and at the absolute lowest cost to her. All of this is to say that globalization has altered the face of the retail landscape, and just as consumers have adjusted to the new global marketplace, so must your company learn to navigate this wild and uncharted terrain.

You can begin by taking small steps. For example, if you offer your products online, take into account that it might no longer be sufficient for your company to market only to your core consumers. After all, you now are selling to a global consumer base, so you must market your merchandise accordingly. Similarly, whereas you most likely already have an in-depth understanding of your local competition, keep in mind that when you begin to sell your products internationally, your company will be faced with the task of competing with businesses from around the globe for consumer dollars, so you may need to identify innovative ways to differentiate your products from those of your new global rivals. But at all times throughout the enterprise of selling your merchandise internationally, proceed with caution.

I'm obviously not saying that expanding your selling internationally is a bad business decision. After all, doing so seems to be almost a prerequisite for staying competitive in a marketplace that is growing ever more global, and for many companies, selling beyond the strictures of their national market has helped them achieve enormous growth. Furthermore, once a company goes global, it will have the opportunity to sell its products in an entirely new environment to a much wider audience of consumers, and it may even benefit from attributable improvements in both the cost efficiency of its business and the diversity of its distribution. But for some companies, global expansion is the equivalent of the kiss of death. Simply put, some companies become so distracted by the temporary growth their businesses enjoy after they have globalized their selling efforts that they begin to predominately concentrate on further expanding internationally, to the detriment of their core business. So few companies are disciplined enough to separate out their commitment to growing globally from their responsibility to improving their core business, and all too often their inadvisable lack of focus on their core growth comes back later in one form or another to haunt them.

Even companies that are incredibly commercially successful find it difficult to leverage several different business game plans at the same time. Take Crocs, for example. Crocs manufactures and distributes a line of footwear that can best be described as synthetic rubber clogs. The shoes themselves, most of which feature large perforations in their uppers for breathability and heel straps to keep them secured to wearers' feet, are not particularly stylish. In fact, they are so entirely deficient in terms of style that, in sales parlance, Crocs shoes would fall under the merchandising category of "bulldog products," or goods that appeal to consumers because they're so ugly that they're actually cute—like a bulldog. But their duckbill-like looks matter not to consumers who place a high priority on the comfort level of their footwear, because what these shoes are lacking in runway appeal they more than make up for in wearability and cushioning.

The unique design and above-average comfort level of its foot-wear have conferred to Crocs a dedicated following of core consumers, but the company was not content to remain a niche brand serving a niche group assortment of buyers. It had its sights set on global expansion. Crocs wanted households worldwide to know about, buy, and love its footwear, so it developed a two-tiered product plan that it hoped would increase the growth of its business operations. The first component of its growth plan involved rolling out its footwear to a wider distribution base, and Crocs tackled this phase of its plan by strategizing ways to begin selling directly to its consumers. Crocs consequently opened up its first flagship retail location in Santa Monica, California, which soon thereafter was followed by store openings in New York and Boston, and it also launched a digital storefront through which to sell its product offerings. Then, to fulfill the second aspect of its expansion plan, which entailed reaching beyond the success of its bull-dog product into more product offerings, Crocs began designing and selling a wider variety of footwear, including flip-flops, wedge sandals, loafers, and boat shoes.

Despite Crocs' growth efforts, however, business began to taper off. Although the company had enjoyed great commercial success in the United States, consumers from other parts of the world were not as enthusiastic about the synthetic rubber clogs as Americans were, and not even Crocs' expanded product range was enough to generate global interest in its footwear lines. Moreover, whereas many consumers initially were happy to purchase Crocs' goofy-looking yet unique clogs purely out of the desire to own such a comfortable pair of shoes, when the company began offering more traditional footwear options, it opened itself up to a world of competition from shoemakers who had been in the flip-flop, loafer, or boot business far longer than Crocs had. Competition also increased soon after Crocs reached a level of mainstream success, when copycat companies came out in droves, offering their knockoff Crocs at bottom-of-the-barrel prices and in locations worldwide. While Crocs was able to fight off some of the competition from these copycat manufacturers and retailers, thanks to the high level of marquee brand status that it had established for itself in its infancy, the company still lost a good portion of potential revenue to knockoffs of Crocs. There were also unexpected drawbacks that Crocs experienced when it began distributing its products to a wider variety of retailers. The shoemaker actually did a fantastic job of stretching the scope of its distribution efforts, but in broadening the availability of its products, it became so easy for consumers to purchase Crocs that the footwear lost some of its early exclusivity appeal. As the brand migrated worldwide and became increasingly obtainable at all sorts of retailers, as well as online and at Crocs stores and kiosks, the footwear grew ever more vulnerable to overexposure.

Crocs didn't necessarily do the wrong thing when it expanded the availability of its shoes. Doing so was an all-important factor that enabled the company not only to sustain its volume but also to gain brand recognition. Where Crocs erred was that it failed to institute a strong global sales strategy that would buoy the company as it reached beyond its initial distribution levels and began offering a wider array of product offerings. As a result, Crocs suffered the loss of its brand diversity, and its footwear evolved away from the mainstream product it once was. Instead, it became a line of shoes that appeals more often to youth and those working in the service industry. Many consumers who owned one pair of Crocs never bought another style or color of the footwear simply because the brand's limited sales concept was never successfully developed in a way that would encourage future purchases.

So, the question that crops up after reading about Crocs' exploits and missteps is: Can a one-dimensional success story profitably expand its reach and gain traction with global consumers? After all, even though it was able to design a creative core product, execute a banner initial product rollout, and build itself a favorable brand image when it was only a young company, ultimately Crocs still fell short of its goal of global expansion and was unable to elevate its brand to a higher and more diverse level. But despite the many setbacks that Crocs experienced in its efforts to go global, I still would say yes to the question raised. As long as a brand creates a core foundation for sustained success, the value of that brand will know no limits, and its volume and worldwide repute will be able to grow by leaps and bounds.

While global branding certainly is of heightened importance in today's increasingly international marketplace, I am concerned that brands big and small will begin devoting so much of their resources and brain power to the pursuit of worldwide growth that they will stunt their internal development. If companies want to brand themselves successfully at the global level, they first and foremost will need to maintain their focus on their core business, always devising new ways to keep consumers engaged with their brand. Especially given today's tough economic environment, companies need to learn how to grow in a controlled manner, and they should never prioritize volume at the expense of their core business. It is essential that you remember to *never* sell your core brand short. Even if the global marketplace seems to be demanding that you evolve beyond your core business, it is critical that you do so only after making a conscious decision based on absolute need.

CHAPTER | **8**

Shift to Accessories

Although the challenging economic climate of 2008–2009 has resulted in a serious consumption slump, the one type of product that consumers have continued to purchase with aplomb, more so than any other, is the accessory. Even during the 2008 holiday shopping season, which as I've noted previously in this book was one of the worst holiday retail environments on record, consumers demonstrated a concerted interest in accessories, purchasing these items in droves to supplement the more expensive "investment" products they already owned. So consumers purchased fashion accessories, electronic accessories, accessories for their homes and even for their cars, while big-ticket items, like plasma televisions and laptop computers, simply gathered dust on retailers' shelves.

One of the more popular accessory purchases during the holiday 2008 shopping season came in the form of video game add-ons. Despite the fact that none of the major video game manufacturers released a new game console that holiday season, consumers were definitely interested in purchasing accessories for the game consoles that they already owned. The Wii Fit, for example, which is an exercise-focused video game bundle developed by Nintendo as a peripheral to its Wii gaming system, proved to be the perfect accessory for consumers who appreciate video games that work out more than just their thumbs. Consisting of a series of interactive exercise regimens and the Wii Balance Board, the Wii Fit met with tremendous commercial success during the 2008 holiday season and helped consumers get even more out of their Nintendo Wii investment.

As the Wii Fit example so aptly demonstrates, consumers today aren't content to merely purchase investment items and then move on to their next big-ticket buys. Rather, they are programmed to enhance and build upon their investment purchases with all manner of upgrades and accessories in an attempt to extract as much value from these products as possible. Just look at how so many consumers approach their electronics purchases. Consumers can't just buy a big-screen television. No, they need a top-of-the-line surround-sound system to perfectly accompany their new television's high-definition picture. Some consumers won't stop accessorizing their new television until their recreation rooms are outfitted with those special theater-style reclining chairs, complete with built-in cup holders. After all, no home theater is complete without them! And don't desktop and laptop computers need to be accessorized, too? First, consumers will go out and buy the essentials, like a hard disk drive, but just how much memory should it be able to store? Then they'll want to upgrade their monitor, but how many inches should it be? And should it be a CRT (cathode ray tube) monitor or an LCD (liquid crystal display) flat panel? And aren't FireWire cables faster than USB (Universal Serial Bus) cords? By the time consumers have finished installing all manner of printers, cameras, and software packages onto their state-of-the-art home computing system, they will have memorized the Geek Squad's customer service number!

Brands and retailers will need to rethink their selling strategies before they will be able to take advantage of consumers' growing fondness for accessory items. After all, accessories often are less expensive than the investment items they are bought to complement, so your company will need to strategize what steps it will take to remain competitive during a time in which consumers are spending less and less money per accessory purchase in stores. One option that many in the fashion industry have exercised to their advantage has been raising the prices of accessories to the extent that they often are some of the most expensive items in designers' clothing lines. In former times, the fashion industry's main investment items were outfits, like dresses and suits, and consumers would later add accessories to their ensembles in order to better express their own personal styles. Today, however, handbags and sunglasses and shoes rapidly are becoming the main attraction in the fashion equation, and in some cases these items even are outpricing and outshining everything else that the consumer is wearing. Gone are the days when the outfit was the primary focal point of an ensemble. Instead, consumers are peering into their closets, assessing the pieces of clothing they already own, and then are purchasing new accessories to complement and breathe new life into their older outfits. Thanks to consumers' penchant for accessories, the outfit has been relegated to secondary status. It has become the accessory to the accessory.

The fashion industry's emphasis on accessories has grown so exaggerated that in many cases consumers with average incomes will reach far beyond their means in order to afford luxury accessory items. Just look at the handbag phenomenon that has swept women off their feet. Women have been carrying the handbag business to new heights with their purchases of big, slouchy totes whose prices are anything but slouchy. And their passion—their gusto!—for these bags is a sight to behold. One day, as I was walking around Central Florida, I spotted a woman who was handling her handbag as though it were her firstborn child. When I asked her why she was clutching on to her bag so tightly, she actually started to cry tears of passion! She explained to me that never in her wildest dreams did she ever believe that she actually would be the proud owner of this particular handbag. As we talked she informed me that she still had not yet revealed to her husband just how expensive her handbag actually had been, and then she asked me whether I thought she was justified in not sharing its price with him. I gently tried to suggest that perhaps she rethink her priorities, but I'm no psychologist. A consumerologist, maybe, but certainly not a psychologist!

On another occasion I happened upon a husband and wife who were busy looking at handbags together. Perhaps I should rephrase that: I happened upon a husband and wife who were busy getting into an *argument* over handbags together. When the wife showed her husband the handbag she was interested in buying, his response was almost formulaic: "But you have one just like it!" His wife predictably gasped in horror at his ignorance, then looked over at me and asked, "Did you just hear the comment that he made?" Enter the industry analyst onto the scene, though of course at the time they had no idea who I was. For my part, I came to the poor husband's rescue and explained to his wife that I was sure her husband simply didn't realize that the very bag she had just then presented to him was the latest Michael Kors tote. Perhaps he had just looked at it from the wrong angle and had missed the logo on the front of the bag. Of course he had made an error, I told her, but a forgivable one at that. The husband sheepishly glanced my way, as if to say "thank you for saving me," and the wife was so shocked that I actually had understood the "importance" of her bag that her mouth dropped wide open in astonishment.

I laughed and finally introduced myself to the couple, and then I asked the husband and wife a few of the questions that I typically inquire of the shoppers that I encounter on my "mall tours." As I interviewed them both, I quickly discovered that while the husband was fairly familiar with his wife's love of handbags, he apparently hadn't realized just how deeply her passions ran. She was so passionate about handbags, in fact, that she admitted during the course of our interview to owning about 30 designer bags. And the moment his wife let this confession slip through her lips, the amiable expression on the husband's face disintegrated into one of shock. He had had absolutely no inkling that his wife owned so many handbags! He had never seen his wife's handbags all in one place and was surprised to learn that she was storing them in the laundry room—the one room in their house the husband admitted he never entered.

While the wife's admission that she had amassed no fewer than 30 handbags had jolted her husband, to say the least, I was not as surprised. The passion, the hidden collection, and the one partner left unaware ... this scenario plays itself out time and time again in my interviews with consumers, which suggests that passion has become an increasingly influential aspect of their purchasing behavior. As was the case with the wife and her handbags, some consumers are so intensely and sincerely passionate about acquiring certain items that they will put themselves—and sometimes their families—at financial risk in order to sate their desires. And handbags aren't the only drivers of such extreme desire in today's marketplace. From fashion products to video games, from beauty supplies to sporting goods, and from designer home goods to consumer electronics, each and every one of these products enjoys its fair share of frenzy-fueled purchases. And as coincidence would have it, the common thread that ties these passionate purchases together is that they are all accessory items.

Don't misunderstand me: I am not suggesting that these are the only types of consumer goods that are capable of eliciting strong emotional reactions from buyers. To be sure, different kinds of consumers are drawn to different kinds of products, as evidenced by all the individuals I have met who are passionate about salt shakers, cat pillows, rooster sculptures, timepieces, scales, you name it. But when it comes to the sorts of merchandise that fall into the aforementioned product categories, consumers just can't help themselves. Their brains may tell them that it's a bad idea to charge yet another handbag or bottle of perfume or video game to their credit card, but who can listen to reason when their heart is saying, "Spend! Spend! Spend!" After all, when consumers are passionate about a product, there's no end to their hunger for more, more, more.

My colleagues and I at NPD were so fascinated by consumers' seemingly limitless passion for fashion accessories in particular that we began administering these buyers a questionnaire to study their purchasing behavior. One of the questions that we asked consumers who had bought a given accessory was whether they had done so impulsively or if they had planned the purchase. Their responses were telling. Take a look at Figure 8.1, which illustrates just how many consumers purchase accessories impulsively—or passionately, if you will—as compared to how many do so only after having planned out their purchases.

So, we have determined that a large percentage of consumers who purchase accessories do so emotionally, but what about those who exercise a certain amount of practicality in their purchasing behavior? What do these consumers look for in a potential accessory purchase? These are two increasingly important questions for companies to be asking themselves during today's rocky economic times, when consumers' overdrawn bank accounts are reigning in even the strongest of purchasing passions. No longer can companies assume that the only two thoughts running through shoppers' heads are: "How quickly can I get this?" and "I have to have this!"

Women's Jewelry Impulse Purchases

Type of Purchase	Dollars ('000)	Dollar Share
Planned Purchase	$1,839,726	43.9%
Not Planned	$2,348,888	56.1%
Not Specified	$0	0.0%

Source: NPD/Consumer Tracking Service

Figure 8.1 Impulse Purchase Tracking

No, today's consumers are assessing their purchases according to an entirely new set of guidelines. They want products that will fill their preexisting needs and make their lives better. They want to know if they really need your products, if it's the right time to purchase them, and if your offerings will enhance the investment items that they already own. But here's a little secret, just between you and me: even though they have been exercising more caution in their purchasing behavior as of late, consumers cannot help but fall prey to their purchasing passions from time to time. They always have, and they always will. So sprinkle a little bit of passion into your offerings. After all, as the woman who accumulated 30 handbags would tell you, a little bit of passion can go a long, long way.

CHAPTER 9

Seasonless Merchandising

Retailers have grown increasingly more disconnected from their consumers, and there is perhaps no better indicator of this swelling chasm than the treatment of seasonal merchandise in the retail environment. I continually am amazed at how poorly retailers synchronize their season merchandise rollouts with the onset of consumers' desire for said products. Since when did the majority of consumers need swimwear in February? Do that many people really plan on going swimming in February? Is there some statistic that I'm not aware of that suggests that an inordinate number of consumers plan their resort vacations for February? How many men and women really want to try on swimwear when their legs are as white as the snow-covered ground outside? And just how many people do retailers expect will loosen their already tight budgets for a piece of clothing that they aren't even going to think about putting on for another two to three months?

Despite all evidence to the contrary, retailers aren't purposefully making consumers' lives harder for them when they offer them swimwear during a time of year when most shoppers are so focused on staying warm that they'd rather go all year without purchasing a new swimsuit than extract themselves from their many layers of clothing to try one on. Retailers offer swimwear in February—and heavy knit shirts in July, and winter coats in September, and so on—because they believe that their consumers are so fashion-focused that they will buy their clothing one season ahead of time just so they can be the first to own a product, flaunt a style, or start a trend. Furthermore, while it's debatable that consumers are as fashion-forward as retailers have assumed them to be (in fact, only about 7 to 10 percent of fashion consumers are preseason purchasers), it's certainly no question that retailers constantly are trying to stay one step ahead of the curve and be the first to offer the latest styles to consumers. They want their products to occupy the most prime real estate on the sales floor, and they want their mall storefront to be the first to display the fashion trends that will characterize the upcoming season's offerings. In short, retailers invariably are trying to boost their sales by being first to the seasonal punch.

It's understandable why retailers think that selling all manner of clothing items months before they are needed will improve their gross revenue. After all, the early bird gets the worm, right? Well, no. Wrong—at least in this case. In fact, consumers are more likely to buy a product in season today than they have been in the past 20 years. So, how could retailers today think it even remotely logical that offering consumers goods a full season before they actually need them will result in banner seasonal sales? Have retailers not noticed how consumers are buying products on an as-needed basis instead of rushing to spend money that they don't have on items that they won't use for months? Have they not realized that consumers care more about day-to-day survival than they do about how great a swimsuit will look on them in three months? Who knows what retailers today are thinking? But I can say for certain what they *aren't* thinking about: giving consumers what they want instead of what retailers want to give them. Retailers have become so entrenched in their habit of offering seasonal products months before consumers realistically can use them that, year after year, seasonal merchandise makes its grand appearance on the sales floor earlier ... and earlier ... and earlier.

So just how disconnected have retailers grown from their consumers? Here's an equation to ponder: The majority of specialty and department stores is selling their fashion-forward merchandise, which constitutes 80 percent of their entire inventories, to the mere 10 percent of the consumer population who actually wants these goods. I think I must be missing something here. I understand what retailers are trying to do. When retailers sell a product forward, they simply are trying to create a longer sales life for that particular item. And part of being a leader in the fashion industry means offering the latest styles before your competition does. When leaders in the fashion industry are the first out of the gates to display a specific type of skirt or suit in their storefronts, they can influence the apparel buys of other retailers in the sector. And many stores don't *really* expect that they will be able to sell all their early receipts at full price. I know these retailers plan all along to sell the majority of their seasonal items at reduced or markdown prices. But ... Haven't they gotten the formula backward? Wouldn't it make more sense for retailers to wait to release their seasonal items into the marketplace until they knew for certain that consumers were ready for them? Wouldn't they ostensibly be able to sell more full-priced seasonal goods this way?

Bathing suits, snow boots, down parkas, and sundresses are not the only seasonal goods that retailers push in front of consumers' noses before they're ready to start smelling. Who among us hasn't walked into their local superstore in October to see Christmas- and Hanukkah-themed merchandise displayed one aisle over from Halloween candy? But alternately, who among us has sauntered into a major retailer on August 18 only to find that it is setting up its end-of-the-year holiday decorations and goods? Well, actually, two years ago, when I walked into the Macy's in Manhasset, New York, I did. I couldn't believe it. The temperature was still 85-plus degrees outside, but here Macy's was, assembling a veritable winter wonderland and preparing for a holiday that was more than four months away. Who, I asked myself, could possibly be interested in shopping for the year-end holiday season in the *middle of August*? But sure enough, over the course of the next two weeks, more and more stores began setting up their holiday shops and shelving the latest decorations, ornaments, varieties of fruitcake, and other "nifty gifties."

Why do stores set up so early for the holiday season? If you think back to why fashion retailers begin offering winter coats months before the year's first snowfall, I'll bet you'll begin to understand why. Just like fashion retailers prefer to preempt the onset of the upcoming season by a few months in order to give their clothing lines as long a full-priced shelf life as possible, so too do stores that carry holiday merchandise. These retailers figure that if they begin selling their holiday goods earlier in the year, they will have sold more full-priced products by the time they are forced to mark down their merchandise than they would have had they started their selling efforts even two weeks later. Additionally, remember how fashion retailers race to become the first store to brandish the "it" style for the upcoming season? Many holiday retailers do the exact same thing. Thinking that holiday shoppers intuitively will turn to them for their holiday shopping needs if they are the first store in the area to offer holiday-themed décor and merchandise, these retailers desperately try to outpace one another in their quest for the honorific title of "holiday retail headquarters."

All in all, the motivating factors behind retailers' decision to start releasing their holiday merchandise earlier and earlier each year are understandable. But when stores begin crowding their shelves with holiday merchandise in August and September, they ultimately do so to the detriment of their overall business. After all, when stores are so entirely enmeshed in the process of promoting ornaments, menorahs, and mistletoe, how can they possibly pay the proper amount of attention to other concurrent—and perhaps better-timed—seasonal promotions, which most likely would drive sales more efficiently in late summer than holiday merchandise would? Consider back-to-school merchandise, for example. Wouldn't it make sense that shoppers would be more inclined to purchase backpacks, crayons, and new wardrobes for their children in late August than they would be to buy a holiday wreath that they'll probably just stuff into their attics?

Regardless of what I think, Sears and its subsidiary retailer Kmart both planned "Christmas in July" store promotions for 2009. Yes, the holidays definitely arrived early for shoppers visiting these two retailers in the balmy summer of 2009! In fact, they arrived approximately five-and-a-half months early, as both retailers had already begun selling their holiday merchandise online and in stores by the time mid-July rolled around. When asked why, exactly, they were rolling out their holiday merchandise so early, Sears and Kmart predictably explained that their "Christmas in July" promotions were designed to help them get a leg up on their competition and to show consumers just how serious they were about the holiday 2009 shopping season.

Before I sound too insensitive, I want to clarify that I don't think "Christmas in July" is all bad. In fact, many consumers even benefit from the layaway programs that generally accompany these in-store promotions. Say a father wants to give his daughter a new bicycle for Christmas. He can visit Kmart in July, pick out a bike for his daughter, and then pay down its cost in the months leading up to December to ensure that come Christmas morning, his daughter will be able to open just the present she had been hoping for. Now, I would not want to deny that little girl of her happiness, nor would I deny the father the experience of seeing his daughter's face light up with glee. But I do worry that the "Christmas Creep," the retail nickname for stores' tendencies to set up their holiday merchandise earlier each year, is quickly turning into the "Christmas Collision." Indeed, when retailers start to focus their selling efforts on holiday goods as early as July, the holiday season can't help but collide with other seasonal promotions that retailers may be running. Eventually, if stores continue to steadily step forward the rollout dates of their holiday merchandise, these products will end up being sold year-round—which is certainly not my idea of good seasonal selling.

I recently visited a number of retailers to survey their various approaches for enticing back-to-school shoppers into their stores. Some stores were primed and ready for the upcoming selling season and were touting the full force of their back-to-school products on their sales floors. Others were simply promoting their usual discounts and merchandise. Some were even offering additional savings on already reduced prices. There was one store in particular, however, whose back-to-school promotion was especially alluring. When I stepped into this store, I was greeted with a tidy and vibrantly colorful sales floor, a caring and attentive staff, and a range of product that was exceptionally applicable for the region and retail location of the store, which was situated at an outlet center in Hilton Head, South Carolina. So, with these clues in mind, do you have any guesses as to which store caught my eye as the clear winner of the back-to-school shopping season for product assortment, presentation, lighting, neatness, clarity of signage, pricing, and overall appeal? It was none other than Nautica, and as I walked through that outlet store that day, I couldn't help but feel as though its back-to-school promotion exemplified some of the early lessons I learned while I was earning my stripes at Bloomingdale's.

Back when I was in college, I began working on a part-time basis in Tysons Corner, Virginia, at what at the time was the only Bloomingdale's located outside of the New York metropolitan area. I was hired before the store had even opened its doors to business, and one of my first responsibilities was to design the men's sweater wall. Did I mention that I had to do so during the scorching heat of August in what can best be described as the swamplands surrounding Washington, D.C.? This was no small task. I mean, this was *Bloomingdale's*! In the *1970s*! And I was working with *wool*. In 95-degree August heat! Sure, I was given the finest of men's Shetland sweaters to work with, which were huge revenue drivers for Bloomingdale's at the time, but given that the odds were stacked against me, how could I possibly design the sweater wall in a way that would draw in consumers?

Nevertheless, I set about to the task of making that sweater wall sing, and I took Bloomingdale's motto as my own—I was going to make it like no other. I had 29 colors to work with to turn a wall of shelves into an eye-popping, show-stopping display, and I worked throughout the night to create that sweater wall, steeled by my desire to turn the head of every last person passing through that store. I finished the sweater wall late at night, but at 7:30 a.m. the following day, my department manager called me up to ask me how quickly I would be able to get back to the store. I tentatively asked him if anything was the matter, and he replied that he urgently needed to speak with me about what I had been working on in the store the night before. Figuring that my manager wanted to reprimand me for my sweater wall, I put off what I thought was the inevitable and told him that I could return to the store no earlier than 4 p.m. I walked into Bloomingdale's at 4 p.m. and looked back proudly at my sweater wall. But as I made my way further into the store and caught sight of my department manager, who was surrounded by a whole host of Bloomingdale's bigwigs, my confidence drained away. As luck would have it, the corporate executives of Bloomingdale's had arrived that day to check out the store just prior to its grand opening and review it case by case, rack by rack, and wall by wall, and I had walked onto the sales floor in the midst of their grand tour. I watched them from a distance until suddenly my department manager noticed me out of the corner of his eye, stopped one of the Bloomingdale's hotshots, and pointed at me.

Mouth agape, I looked on in awe as the entire group of executives turned and started walking toward me, and as they drew nearer and nearer, I suddenly realized that one of the men accompanying my department manager was the president of Bloomingdale's—Marvin Traub! As if I weren't nervous enough, here was a true retail legend walking my way! The group of bigwigs closed in on me, and Mr. Traub stepped out in front and asked me if I was Marshal Cohen. I nodded yes. I couldn't find my voice, but at least I could nod! By this point in time, I was obviously perspiring, so to make light of my nervousness, Mr. Traub then said to me, "Must be hot out there, huh? We appreciate you running over, but you didn't have to *literally* run here." He put his hand out to shake mine, and then he put his arm around me and led me over in the direction of the sweater wall. *My* sweater wall. We stood in front of my display, his hand on my elbow, and he turned me toward the wall and began asking me a series of questions about why I had chosen to display the Shetland sweaters in the way that I had. Finally, Mr. Traub turned to his entourage and said, "Put this guy on the fast track! This is the best display of color merchandising I have ever seen. This is the new standard that this store must meet, and not a single merchandising display meets up to these standards." Imagine my relief! Mr. Traub proceeded to ask me when I would graduate from college, and then told me that the day after I graduated, I was to come directly to his office and he would personally see to it that I was enrolled in Bloomingdale's highly selective Leadership Development Program. Fortunately those wool sweaters sold like crazy!

Thanks to the plushness of those Shetland sweaters, the perfect folding trick I had employed, and the array of colors I was given to work with, that sweater wall popped like fireworks on the Fourth of July. But the moral of this story isn't just about me, my career, and Merchandising 101. It's also about understanding how to merchandise your products so that your consumers feel a sense of connection to them—even if it's 95 degrees outside and you're trying to sell them sweaters! My own little sweater wall in Tysons Corner, Virginia, proved that wool could be sold year-round if retailers simply highlighted those sweaters with softer, more flowery colors in their spring and summer displays. I learned that color could be used as a lure to evoke specific seasonal feelings in consumers, and in doing so I took seasonality out of the equation for Shetland wool sweaters, which became comfort items for consumers looking to combat the chill of air conditioning or a cool late-summer evening. So be conscious of what it is that you're trying to sell, as well as when you're trying to sell it, and you might just have a sweater wall epiphany of your own. After all, if a college kid could turn Shetland wool sweaters into a seasonless product, then you can too.

Gender Bender

After the Bloomingdale's store in Tysons Corner, Virginia, opened for business, I moved on from designing the department store's sweater walls and began selling its men's sportswear and tailored clothing. I was proud of my department and served my shoppers with the understanding that I was offering them the market's best selection of merchandise, presented in an appealing way and at a fair price. But now that I think back to my time in that particular department, I realize that my team and I never really focused our attention on who was actually buying our menswear products. Sure, we paid a lot of attention to our weekly sales reports and would comb through them to identify which products sold best, which stores were running low on inventory, and the like. But nowhere in our weekly sales reports did we identify who the main purchasers of our products were. Being the inquisitive soul that I am, I decided to make it my business to find out.

I started to pay closer and closer attention to the types of consumers to whom I was selling Bloomingdale's menswear. Then one day, after selling yet another piece of neckwear to a female shopper, who had purchased it for a man in her life, it hit me: could it be possible that women were shopping for men more often than men were shopping for themselves? I asked my fellow coworkers to join in on my field research and track how many of our menswear buyers—and not just shoppers, mind you, but buyers—were male versus how many of them were female. What we discovered was astonishing. As it turned out, my hunch that a disproportionate amount of women were shopping for men was more on point than I could have ever possibly imagined. On the day that my team took its tally, almost 75 percent of the menswear purchasers had been women! And this phenomenon is not just limited to Bloomingdale's shoppers. In fact, female heads of households are the primary purchasers of all kinds of products, from men's underwear to wallets to laundry detergent. The most important lesson that my team and I took away from the informal survey we took in the menswear department at Bloomingdale's that month was that we had been marketing our products to the wrong shopper. We had spent so much time observing the male shopper, learning his likes and dislikes, and working with manufacturers and designers to create the perfect mix of men's attire in our department that we had totally overlooked an entire demographic of consumers who were purchasing our products.

The knowledge that I gained as a young man while working and observing the consumers who browsed the menswear department at Bloomingdale's has served me quite well throughout my career. For example, I recall reviewing Ralph Lauren's upcoming clothing line one season and asking his designers if their menswear products would be available in any other colors. When they informed me that they wanted the look of their newest men's line to be more muted in color, I said, "That's nice, but I need to see these clothes in colors that women would like." They looked at me like I had two heads growing out of my neck, so I explained to them why I thought expanding the color offerings of their newest line would be a worthwhile endeavor, and the designers agreed to try out the concept. Together we softened their collection's emphasis on traditional menswear patterns, opting instead for brighter, more "feminine" colors, new prints, and bolder patterns that would differentiate their men's clothing from the competition. Needless to say—since I am writing about our adventure!—Ralph Lauren's menswear line sold briskly that season, which revealed to me that retailers would need to rethink who, exactly, was actually purchasing their products and then begin tailoring their buying and marketing efforts to that demographic of shoppers. In essence, retailers would have to engage in a little something I like to call retail "gender bending."

The lessons that Ralph Lauren's designers and I learned about gender marketing are no less relevant today than they were 30 years ago. In fact, as recently as 2007 I *still* was talking to audiences about the sorry extent to which certain markets—specifically electronics—catered their products and marketing efforts to men. At that time in retail history, the vast majority of electronics purchases were being made by male consumers, but Best Buy wisely realized that if it took a few simple yet strategic steps to woo in female consumers, it could potentially double its volume of sales. So Best Buy opened up its Studio D concept store, which was designed to offer female consumers a more user-friendly, lower-stress, and overall more comfortable electronics shopping experience. This boutique Best Buy was outfitted with sofas and bistro cafés, and its employees even wore pink polo shirts in place of Best Buy's trademark blue ones!

While the Studio D concept store, which was located in Naperville, Illinois, eventually was closed down, Best Buy's efforts to provide women with a female-friendly environment in electronics retail stores should serve as the model against which retailers across industries revamp their sales outreach. After all, more and more women are making the purchasing decisions in their households and as such are managing a number of tasks that once were the purview of men (Figure 10.1). From electronics and vacation packages to grills and automobiles, women are now in charge of purchasing them all, and the first step that savvy retailers will take to adapt to this new gender-bending reality is to design and market their products not only for their end users but also for the purchasers of their products.

**Family Groups With Children Under 18 Years Old,
by Race and Hispanic Origin: 1980 to 1998**

Race and Hispanic origin of householder or reference person	Percent distribution			
	1980	1990	1995	1998
All races, total [1]	100	100	100	100
Two-parent family groups	79	72	69	68
One-parent family groups	22	28	31	32
Maintained by mother	19	24	26	26
Maintained by father	2	4	5	6
White, total	100	100	100	100
Two-parent family groups	83	77	75	73
One-parent family groups	17	23	25	27
Maintained by mother	15	19	21	21
Maintained by father	2	4	4	6
Black, total	100	100	100	100
Two-parent family groups	48	39	36	38
One-parent family groups	52	61	64	62
Maintained by mother	49	56	58	57
Maintained by father	3	4	6	5
Hispanic, total [2]	100	100	100	100
Two-parent family groups	74	67	64	64
One-parent family groups	26	33	36	36
Maintained by mother	24	29	31	30
Maintained by father	2	4	5	6

[1] Includes other races, not shown separately. [2] Hispanic persons may be of any race.

Source: U.S. Census Bureau, *Current Population Reports*, P20-515, and earlier reports; and unpublished data.

Figure 10.1 U.S. Census Bureau data indicating growth in one parent families and families maintained by mothers.

Of course, some companies are savvier than others. Consider the automobile industry, for example. A number of automakers have recognized the power of the female purchaser and have begun to tailor their cars, marketing messages, and sales strategies to this growing demographic of consumers. And while many car companies certainly have fallen short in their outreach efforts, others, like Toyota, Lexus, and Saturn, consistently receive high ratings from female consumers, who feel that these brands focus on and address their car buying needs more so than any other. Cadillac, too, has taken measures to grab the attention of female consumers by releasing brilliant advertising campaigns that speak to their purchasing wants and desires. In one of Cadillac's more memorable female-centric ads, the camera zooms in on the actress Kate Walsh, who assures watchers that buying a car these days isn't a question of sunroofs or pop-up navigation screens. "No," she says, "the real question is, when you turn your car on, does it return the favor?" And Cadillac has done more than simply air advertisements that break from the traditional, male-focused car commercial mold. By pinpointing who was actually buying its cars, Cadillac—just like Best Buy, Toyota, Lexus, and Saturn—beat the gender rules and was able to design, market, and sell its products to all-powerful female purchasers.

Indeed, an entirely new set of purchasing rules is emerging in the retail environment, and companies that acclimate to this dramatic shift in purchasing protocol by overhauling their sales and marketing techniques and expanding their target audiences to include female as well as male consumers will enjoy the fruits of their labors in their bottom lines. Just look at how many industries have grown substantially after opening their marketing channels to both genders. The beauty industry, once considered the exclusive domain of female consumers, bent the gender rules and began marketing and distributing products designed specifically for men and, well, the numbers speak for themselves. In 2007, the first year that beauty companies really turned their attention to the needs and desires of male consumers, men's grooming products were the fastest growing segment in beauty products, boasting a 5 percent increase in sales. The home improvement industry too has variegated its product offerings, and now hammers and drills are finding happy homes with women shoppers, who were drawn to purchase these items thanks to companies like Tomboy Tools, which redesigned them with the female consumer in mind. Even restaurants have been profiting from diversified menu options, like lower-calorie meals and vegetarian plates, which appeal to a wider audience of diners.

While many companies and industries have strategically widened the scope of their product offerings and marketing tactics to entice a broader demographic of shoppers, from time to time consumer demand forces them into gender bending their sales techniques. For example, the sunglasses industry saw an unprecedented and unprovoked surge—around a 10 percent increase—in purchases made by younger males in 2008. What do I mean by *unprovoked*? Sunglasses manufacturers and distributors didn't deliberately target this demographic of consumers. In fact, they didn't do *anything* to draw these young men into their stores. There were no male-focused marketing campaigns, no advertising onslaughts, no new product designs—no nothing. Their mentality was far from "build it and they will come." More accurately, their thought process ran more along the lines of "they are coming, so build it to supply the demand."

An interesting thing happened with young male consumers and sunglasses. Seemingly out of nowhere, sunglasses became *the* must-have image item for these shoppers, who were looking for a low-cost product that would help them make a statement and portray a certain image with their appearance. This generation of young men was buying up big, bold, colorful frames adorned with over-sized designer logos by the handfuls, leaving manufacturers and distributors with no other choice but to catch up with consumer demand and design, produce, and eventually market their sunglasses to these shoppers. Progressive retailers began setting up sunglasses shops front and center in their stores to respond to this growing trend, and even big-name department stores like Bloomingdale's and Saks Fifth Avenue moved their sunglasses into the most prime pieces of real estate their sales floors had to offer.

To be sure, some retailers resisted the sunglasses trend. In fact, one retailer challenged my suggestion that male consumers' desire for sunglasses would remain as red-hot as ever as the retail market swung on into 2009. Now, I know that I'm not infallible, but still,

I couldn't believe that this retailer would deny what was an obvious retail craze. So I decided to do a little digging, and when I looked into my NPD data, I discovered the source of this particular retailer's confusion. Whereas the rest of the market had gender-bent its sales and marketing tactics in an attempt to capitalize on young male consumers' exploding eagerness for sunglasses, this reluctant retailer had stayed its course and had continued to cater its sunglasses sales efforts to female shoppers. No wonder this retailer was skeptical about just how long the sunglasses trend would last! But perhaps my retail prediction did not go unheeded, as sure enough, three months after our initial encounter, I popped over to that same retailer's Web site only to find that the lead product it was featuring was none other than men's sunglasses.

I suppose I understand why this retailer was so reluctant to agree with me that a tidal wave of a trend was swelling in the young male consumer demographic. After all, why would male shoppers have *any* desire—let alone a strong one—to go out and purchase products like sunglasses, which traditionally have been marketed to female consumers? Don't male and female shoppers buy items in response to different trigger points? Well, maybe once upon a time they did. But as the sunglasses example demonstrates, males and females seem to have become more androgynous in their spending habits, effectively eroding the once tried-and-true boundary lines separating these two demographics. And NPD's research backs up this postulation. By NPD's calculations, young females and males are sharing their products, shopping together, and even are declaring a member of the opposite sex as their best friends at increasingly significant rates.

I recently surveyed the hundreds of college students that I teach to see how many of them claim a best friend of the opposite sex, and their response was overwhelming: a whopping 50 percent of these young adults answered that yes, their best friend was a member of the opposite sex. Now compare this feedback to that of a group of students who I surveyed just two years prior, 36 percent of whom indicated that their best friend was of the opposite sex. I'll admit that my research method was not exactly scientific; nevertheless, my students' responses do make me wonder just how often consumers are crossing over traditional gender lines when they are shopping. How often are consumers shopping with members of the opposite sex, and how frequently are their purchasing decisions being influenced by the opinions of their shopping partners? How many products are being shared between two members of opposite sexes? How many close friends are joining forces when they set out to purchase digital cameras, laptops, and other electronics? While there are no hard facts or data available to precisely answer these important questions, it is clear that the old rules of gender-specific marketing no longer apply. So adapt accordingly and speak to your audience in a broader language than you've ever used before, one that connects your company and your products to both males and females.

Take a long, hard look at how you are marketing your products, and never neglect to consider that your target audience may just be more expansive than you initially suspected it to be. After all, consumers are fearless when it comes to crossing gender lines, and it is up to you to discover which of your products and marketing messages you must adapt to cater to this audience of gender-bending consumers. Keep in mind that some of your sales efforts will resonate with males, some will resonate with females, and some will entice consumers of both sexes equally—but don't fall into the trap of thinking that one marketing message will always suffice for everyone. *You* may understand what your marketing outreach is trying to say, but that doesn't mean the rest of your audience will. Even if you've met with success by marketing in the exact same way for decades, the time has come to change your approach. There's a whole new world of consumers out there. Don't you want your company and your products to be what reaches them?

CHAPTER 11

Booming Boomers

When I think about baby boomers, I think about apparel—which is a strange parallel to draw, I know. But hear me out: despite the economic maelstrom that took hold in mid-2008 and raged on throughout much of 2009, baby boomers bought a grand total of $55 billion worth of apparel during the 12-month period that ended in May 2009 and were running only 3 percent behind their sales figures from the prior year. Now compare their numbers for the same time period to those of the younger demographic of 18- to 34-year-olds, who supposedly are more fashion-conscious than their older counterparts. While this younger group of shoppers spent approximately $9 billion more of their hard-earned dollars than did baby boomers, the extent to which their rate of sales lagged as compared to the prior year was right around *double* that of baby boomers. That's right, *double*.

So, now that you know about baby boomers' apparent fondness for apparel, I'm sure you can understand why I have come to view the words "boomer" and "buyer" almost synonymously. By some estimates, baby boomers constitute 26 percent of the overall U.S. population—or 78 million shoppers. And these are not timid consumers. No, the vast majority of the 78 million baby boomers who are alive today are avid shoppers—so avid, in fact, that they account for about 50 percent of all consumer spending. It's no wonder that there's so much literature detailing how to market to this particular demographic of consumers circulating around the book-o-sphere! And to be quite honest, no sales or marketing book, including this one, would be complete if it didn't include some choice tidbits on how to capitalize on the spending power of this booming demographic of baby boomers.

For those of you who don't already know, baby boomers are technically categorized as those adults who were born between the years of 1946 and 1964, but to tell you the truth, their age has little to do with why this demographic of consumers is so unique. Sure, the youngest baby boomer alive today is at least 46 years old, but they certainly don't feel or act like 40- or 50-year-olds. Boomers are looking for ways to look younger, feel younger, and even live younger, and if your company carries products that will help this demographic of consumers keep up the façade of its younger, more virile days, you had better let them know. Otherwise, you may never be able to fully appreciate just how powerful the spending power of this generation can be.

Opportunities abound across almost every single industry for companies to successfully market their products to baby boomers, who are trying to buy their way out of the throes of old age. Take the beauty industry, for example, and its anti-aging skin care merchandise, which has found an eager target audience in younger consumers, like the students I teach, who frequently tell me, "I love my mom, but I don't want to look like her when I'm her age." While these younger consumers' words might be painful for their mothers to hear, they sound sweet as can be to retailers of anti-aging skin care products. Indeed, these retailers are thrilled that this younger demographic has turned to their moisturizers, serums, cleansers, you name it, to prevent the crow's-feet and smile lines that they fear will soon creep up on their faces, and they have marketed their products to these shoppers accordingly to great success. In directing their marketing efforts solely to this younger age bracket, however, anti-aging skin care retailers are neglecting the huge percentage of boomer buyers who would purchase their products if only they were positioned differently.

Now, I understand why anti-aging skin care brands focus so much of their marketing attention on younger consumers. After all, these shoppers are buying their products at unprecedented rates and will continue to do so for far longer than aging boomers will. Furthermore, those retailers that do understand the buying power of baby boomers figure that there's no need to adjust their marketing efforts so that it skews to these older shoppers, because, hey, doesn't this crowd think of itself as young *anyway*? But what these anti-aging skin care retailers don't realize is that just because their products benefit two very different types of consumers doesn't mean that both of these demographics will respond in the same way to their marketing outreach—especially when it so obviously is directed to only one of these groups of shoppers. No, one-size advertisements don't fit all anymore. But if retailers merely made a simple adjustment to the way that they currently market their anti-aging skin care products, presenting them not only as preventers of aging but also as preservers of youth, they just might be able to bait both younger *and* older consumers.

The anti-aging skin care business is not the only industry that has misjudged just how enticing its products are to baby boomers. Consider if you will the Element, the really boxy SUV that Honda rolled out onto the car market in 2003. Honda designed the Element specifically with the younger driver in mind, but a funny thing has happened over the course of the five years that it has been on the market. If you've ever thought about purchasing this particular vehicle or have admired it from afar, you've probably noticed a common thread tying its drivers together, and I'll give you a hint as to what it is: they most certainly were not born in the 1970s and 1980s. That's right, baby boomers became entranced with the types of outdoorsy adventures that they envisioned the Honda Element would take them on, and they commandeered it for themselves. Plus, it didn't hurt that the vehicle is incredibly versatile and very easy to get into and out of. Amusingly enough, the marketing team at Honda had no idea that boomers would be drawn so greatly to the Element. In fact, it was so confident that the camperlike appeal and sporty, woodsy feel of the Element would be a hit with younger drivers that their product launch campaign highlighted the vehicle's "kick-ass sound system." Little did they know how big of a home run it would hit with the boomer crowd, "kick-ass sound system" or not! Baby boomers' overwhelmingly positive reaction to the Element revealed to Honda's marketing team that not all bull's-eyes are situated on the target you're aiming for.

So learn from Honda's unintentional missteps, keep an open mind, use your best judgment, and aim high, aim low, aim in any which direction that seems promising. You just might find that your marketing efforts connect with an audience you weren't expecting them to. And never, *ever* discount the spending power of baby boomers. So many brands today are pooh-poohing this group of power spenders and thinking to themselves, "Okay, enough already with the boomers. Let's just move on to the younger shoppers. After all, the youngest of the boomers is *at least* 46 years old. How many more spending years can I really expect to get out of them? Whereas young consumers? I can hook them for life!" But these retailers need to think again. Boomers have more of a tendency to spend, and they certainly have more cash on hand to do so than do younger consumers. What's more, there will be no better group of consumers to have on your company's side as it navigates its way up and out of the economic challenges of 2008–2009 than baby boomers. Now, it might take this older group of shoppers a little more time to recover from the recent economic maelstrom than it will for younger consumers, who will be so tired of curbing their desire to spend that they go hog-wild come the early stages of the economic recovery period. But after they rebuild their confidence—as well as a little bit of their retirement funding—boomers will be right behind them.

So watch out, world! The boomer is coming back to spend. Just don't get in their way as they navigate the new consumption landscape and root out stores and brands that understand and cater to their needs. Or perhaps I should say, *do* get in their way. Let baby boomers know what your company has to offer them by appealing to their needs, desires, and passions, rather than their age. Then watch as these older shoppers pick up where they left off and continue to drive the pulse of consumption up until the very ends of their lives.

Influence the Influencers

Do you realize that almost every single consumer thinks about whether or not the people in his or her life—or even random strangers—will approve of the products that he or she purchases? When a consumer purchases a new car, she thinks, "How will other people perceive me when I roll up to a stoplight in this car?" And when a shopper is choosing between two pairs of jeans, he thinks, "Which of these pairs of jeans will that girl that I like think is more stylish?" Indeed, consumers are constantly seeking feedback on their potential purchases from others. Sometimes they turn to their friends or shopping buddies for advice. Sometimes they ask for the opinions of their family members or colleagues who they know are the "experts" on the products that they are considering buying. And a lot of times consumers simply tune in to one of the morning news television shows to see what the scores of "experts" on air have to say about hairstyles, makeup, clothing, you name it.

But, wait a minute: are you seeing a trend develop here? Because I sure am: more often than not, consumers make the purchasing decisions that they do because they have been influenced in some way to do so. And no matter what form the influencing comes in, its end result is always the same: it motivates. Whether by way of peer pressure or education that is provided by a respected expert or persuasive advertising or some other avenue altogether, influence—more so than almost any other factor—motivates consumers to purchase.

You're no doubt thinking: "Okay, great. But influence is the very reason that we *market* our products to consumers." But not so fast: not every type of consumer is influenced in the same way, so unless your company is rolling out at least three different marketing campaigns for each product that it releases, you're not doing enough to influence your shoppers. Why three, you ask? Well, consumers respond to influence in ways that are unique to their consumption personality, and there just so happen to be three distinct influenced consumption personalities. Let's review them.

The first type of influenced consumer is the *lead consumer*. This consumer is like the kid who would always stay after class to ask the teacher to provide more detailed answers than were given during the lesson. Consumers in this category do their homework, and they like to be out there on their own in the retail environment, discovering the best products, setting the trends, and buying the newest and latest items before anyone else on the block does. Given their tendency to want to be the first to show off to their friends the newest "it" gadget that they have bought, these consumers often are risk takers. They are willing to experiment with new products, and when their risky purchases turn out to be diamonds in the rough, they feel very pleased with themselves, thank you very much! Lead consumers also generally have little qualms about spending more on the products that they buy. After all, who can wait for discounts and sales to be offered when you're constantly trying to stay ahead of the curve? These consumers are rarely swayed by peer pressure—mostly because they are the ones putting the pressure on others to buy the "right" products, the ones that they have already purchased! No doubt you can call to mind one of your friends whom you've sworn off going shopping with because you always end up impulsively buying what she has convinced you are the latest and greatest products on the market. She's a lead consumer, and stores *love* her.

In fact, stores love lead consumers so much that while only 15 percent of all shoppers fall into this consumer category, the vast majority of brands market its products to these trendsetters more than it does to any other group of buyers. What's more, many retailers even develop their product offerings with this group of lead consumers in mind. Brands' and retailers' reasons for focusing so much of their attention on lead consumers are understandable enough. To be sure, these consumers shop earlier, preseasonally, and more frequently than the other consumer types, and they even are the most influential shoppers. But brands sometimes go overboard with their fondness for these shoppers, and many even make the mistake of considering them their core consumers. Well, I suppose they *are* the core consumers for some retailers, but only for around 11 percent of them!

The second type of influenced consumer is the *need consumer*. Remember those folks back in high school who would spend every ounce of their downtime at the mall? You'd run into them every time you had to make a purchase, and you'd beg your mom to let you go underwear shopping by yourself for fear that they'd be there to witness the whole event. More likely than not, those teenagers were need consumers. They shop for fun and to enhance their lives, they shop with friends, and they shop in their leisure time. They shop. And they shop. And they shop. And they most certainly take their time while doing so. After all, need consumers want to feel comfortable with their purchases. They want to know just how much a product can do for them. So, need consumers dig around for information online. They head into store after store in search of the best products at the best prices, which they prefer to be served up with the best customer service. They also seek out the advice of their friends—and they do so more often than any of the three consumer types. They'll then write out a 50-page-long dissertation on their findings. Okay, I'm just kidding about that last one, but you know what I mean. All of need consumers' background research tends to delay the moment when they finally take out their money to pay for the products that they have finally deemed worthy enough to take home with them. Clearly, need consumers buy with a purpose and think twice before committing to any one product. But from time to time, these consumers will shop impulsively, if they are baited properly.

So, how can you entice need consumers to skip over their long deliberation process and simply buy your products on the spot? The key is finding some way to validate what they already believe about themselves: that they are fairly savvy shoppers. Sometimes a one-day sale will persuade need consumers to bypass their drawn-out decision-making process, if the deals that you are offering them are so good that they'll congratulate themselves for finding them in the first place. Other times your most convincing sales associate might be able to provide them with the validation that they so desire. Even spot-on advertisements will incline need consumers to purchase your products without thinking twice, but don't be fooled into thinking that you'll be able to establish any sort of brand loyalty among these types of shoppers. After all, they're just as equally influenced by the advertisements and marketing efforts of your competitors as they are by yours.

More than anything, remember that need consumers enjoy shopping—and they enjoy it even more so when they can share it with others, whether they accompany their friends on their shopping trips or offer up the knowledge they've gained from their many years of retail researching. To be sure, this segment of shoppers loves to hold sway over the purchasing decisions of their friends, family, and colleagues—and they do so better than any other type of consumer. So, if you want to get the most bang for your advertising and marketing bucks, focus on need consumers, who account for 35 percent of all consumers.

The third type of influenced consumer is the *deed consumer*. Maybe you've seen the 2004 movie *Along Came Polly*, starring Ben

Stiller and Jennifer Aniston. Ben Stiller plays a character named Reuben Feffer, who works as a risk manager for an insurance company. But that's not all Reuben does: he is absolutely *neurotic* about risk, and even goes so far as to use his handy-dandy Riskmaster software to weigh the hazards of getting into a relationship with Jennifer Aniston's somewhat flighty, free-spirited character.

When I think back to Ben Stiller's character in *Along Came Polly*, I can't help but think that he would be a deed consumer. After all, those who fall within this group of shoppers are not overly impulsive, and they're certainly not willing to buy a product merely because it received favorable reviews—or so they've *heard*, seeing as how they have little to no interest in doing retail background research themselves. That would be too risky, now, wouldn't it? They also are not interested in being the first in their neighborhood to own a particular product. In fact, they don't so much as know what the newest products or brands on the market are, because they simply don't care—or even really *think*—about shopping.

At best, deed consumers view shopping as a chore and hit the stores only when they have a bona fide reason to do so—and even then, they stick to the retailers they're comfortable with, more so than any other group of shoppers. And generally speaking, the stores and brands that they are most loyal to are those that provide them with the products that they're looking for at the best prices. But watch out if another store or brand starts selling the same or a similar item that you do but at a lower price, because for deed consumers, price trumps store loyalty—and really anything else that retailers have to offer. Even if these shoppers love the taste of your brand of soft drinks more than any other beverage on the market, they would be willing to switch to another company if they could save 20 percent or more by doing so.

That's right, when they do actually go shopping, deed consumers will hop from retailer to retailer—and sometimes even from online storefront to online storefront—until they are able to find the right product and the right price. And when they do find the deal that they were looking for? First they will tell anyone who will listen to them about their major discovery, and then they will sit back and relax until their next shopping foray, glowing with pride the entire time. Perhaps this is the reason why deed consumers demonstrate the penchant for shopping later in the season that they do. After all, there's no better time to find the deal of a lifetime than when hitting up the clearance racks at the end of the season. Now that I think about it, it probably would be more apt for this group of shoppers to be dubbed the deal consumer!

Deed consumers do step out of their Reuben Feffer shopping personas when they see that a celebrity has endorsed the product that they're thinking about buying, but they trust the opinions and advice of their friends and family even more. In fact, these consumers are so susceptible to the influence of others that they'll even try out a new product that they otherwise wouldn't think about buying if someone close to them has recommended that they do so. Deed consumers round out the bottom tier of the consumption pyramid, and as you can see in Figure 12.1, they are by far the largest segment of the consumer types, accounting for over 50 percent of all consumers.

! ! !

Now that we have taken stock of the different types of influenced consumers who are driving today's retail market and hinted at the fact that each distinct category of shoppers impacts the others' shopping behavior, let's take a look at how their influence plays out in real time. During the holiday shopping season of 2008, digital cameras were being scooped up by the dozens, and while the sheer volume of cameras consumers were purchasing was

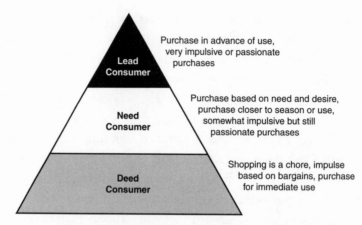

Figure 12.1 Pyramid of Influence

impressive, I found another fact much more interesting. As it turns out, the majority of consumers who were purchasing digital cameras *already had one at home.* When I investigated further, I learned that these camera shoppers weren't purchasing duplicates for themselves; rather, they were purchasing them as holiday gifts for friends or family members. Their families had declared them the official digital camera purchasers of the holiday season because they already owned a digital camera and therefore ostensibly understood better than any of the other relatives which brands offered the best piece of electronics for the best price.

That same holiday season, I went on air to do a preholiday television shot for Fox Business News, and the anchor who was interviewing me, Dagen McDowell, asked me which products would serve as particularly good gifts during the upcoming holiday season. I mentioned a number of items, one of which was digital cameras. Then Dagen shot me a follow-up question and inquired as to whom viewers should purchase these pieces of electronics for, and I told her that the best candidates would be grandmothers. She seemed perplexed, so I explained that because grandmothers' teenaged grandchildren understood digital cameras better than anyone else in their families, they could use their knowledge to their grandmothers' advantage and give them a gift that they couldn't purchase for themselves. Now, as a thought exercise, who do you think fell into the need consumer category: the grandmother or the teenaged grandchild? If you guessed the teenaged grandchild, I have five words for you: Ding, ding, ding, ding, ding! Yes, teenaged grandchildren, or need consumers, were purchasing digital cameras for their grandmothers, or deed consumers, and in the process were opening up these deed consumers to a world they had not really explored before: electronics. Indeed, during the holiday season of 2008, the retail market witnessed need consumers doing what they do best: influencing those shoppers with whom they have the most sway—deed consumers.

Given the overwhelming influence of, well, *influence*, how can stores capitalize on consumers' desire for the approval of others when they make their purchases? Sometimes, if retailers are lucky, their sales staff can occupy the role of the influencer. But as stores opt for less and less expensive—or, in other words, less experienced—sales help, they are finding that their sales associates are not nearly as influential of a factor in consumers' purchasing decisions as they once were. What *does* seem to be consistently working for stores, however, are customer loyalty programs.

Have ever you patronized a store that offers its customers points or rewards when they make a purchase? Even coffee shops leverage this tactic with their "Buy 10 Cups of Coffee and the Next One's on Us" promotions. By simply handing consumers paper cards that are either hole-punched or stamped upon each coffee purchase and then pouring them a free beverage after their tenth cup of joe, coffee shops certainly are breeding brand loyalty. But what about taking the coffee shop concept and going one step further with it? Why not turn your core consumers into influencers by rewarding them for bringing their friends into your store? A simple "Share the Delight, Bring a Friend and Get a Cup on Us" campaign not only will solidify your relationship with your core consumers but also will expand your existing consumer base.

Take a page from the playbook of Direct TV, whose referral program offers existing customers $50 off their bill if they persuade a friend to sign up for its direct broadcast satellite service. If you think Direct TV's referral program doesn't work, think again. After all, how would *you* like to save $50 for simply influencing a friend? Mmm-hmm ... that's what I thought. And if you were the consumer on the influenced end of the purchasing equation, wouldn't you trust a brand or product referral more if it came from a friend or a family member than if it came from an advertisement? I know I would. In fact, the majority of consumers react most strongly to influence if its source is their family members or close friends. Yet, for some reason, brands and retailers alike ignore the power of the influencer and focus solely on their potential buyers. But have they considered just who is driving their sales? Is it the person who merely paid for the purchase or the one who suggested that the item was just right for the purchaser in the first place? I think by now we all know the answer to that question. So why not tap into the two types of influenced consumers who collectively deliver 85 percent of your business and reward the most influential group of shoppers (the need consumers) and the most influenced group of shoppers (the deed consumers)? Don't just sit back, cross your fingers, and hope that consumers will find their own path to you. Lead them to your door by incentivizing the influencer.

Another option that will help you cash in on consumers' desire for the purchasing approval of others is implementing an influence-the-influencer marketing strategy. And lucky for you, it's never been easier to influence the influencer than it is today, thanks to the overwhelming power of social media. Vehicles like MySpace, Facebook, and Twitter have made it incredibly easy for businesses to distribute information about their products and lifestyles to millions of potential consumers with the click of a mouse.

Take Facebook, for example. Say your company decides to create a Facebook page for one of its products. If a consumer buys
your product, uses it, and loves it, she can simply log on to Facebook and become a fan of your product page. After she does so,
Facebook's home page will post an announcement that this particular consumer became a fan of your product, and all 500 of her
Facebook friends will be able to read that she likes your product.
Now suppose that one of her Facebook friends notices that this consumer likes your product and then thinks to himself, "Hey! I like
that product too! I'm going to become a Facebook fan of it as
well." The process repeats itself, and now all 350 of *his* Facebook
friends now know that he likes your product. And I'm sure you can
guess what happens if three of his Facebook friends *also* decide that
they want to become fans of your product. So now, because you
posted a product page to Facebook, you've exposed your product
to at least 850 more consumers than you otherwise would have had
you simply sat on the sidelines and not taken advantage of this
incredibly powerful communications tool. If your company hasn't
already jumped on the social media bandwagon, the time has certainly come for you to do so.

There are literally thousands of ways to leverage social media
marketing to your company's competitive advantage, all of which
reach far more potential consumers and cost thousands of dollars
less than traditional means of advertising. But if you do choose to
go down this path, and I strongly suggest that you do, your social
marketing messaging will only sow what it REAPs. In other words,
it must be Relevant, Exciting, Altering, and Pinpoint-focused.

To break it down, here's what your marketing message must be:

- *Relevant* – It must be important enough to be of interest and
  break through the daily barrage of information congestion.
- *Exciting* – Your message needs to be interesting enough to
  entice users to take the time to read and share it. One-way

conversations aren't exciting, so to increase the likelihood that your message will be passed on, make sure it is informative and readable.

- *Altering* – What aspect of your marketing message will change users' lives for the better? Users don't want to hear that your product is "nice to have." After all, there are plenty of items in the retail marketplace that would be nice to have. Differentiate your product from the rest of the pack by telling users about how your product will make their lives more whole. A new flavor of ice cream isn't necessarily life altering, but a variety that is healthy for you sure is. If you need guidance in this area, I suggest you follow the example of Smart Balance, which has been advertising its fat-free milk by informing consumers that 2 percent milk contains 20 percent more saturated fat than a small serving of French fries. Now *that* is life altering!

- *Pinpoint-focused* – When I wrote my previous book, *Why Customers Do What They Do*, I emphasized the importance of lifestyle marketing, wherein brands would promote the fact that they were the go-to company for a specific niche of products. So, if I was a bike enthusiast, a brand would reel me in by offering me every biking product I could possible want—and then some! But today's consumers are no longer looking for brands to be the be-all and end-all answer that they were just a few years ago. Instead, they want you to pinpoint the best of what you have to offer, and then they want you to tell them about it. So hone in on what it is that you do better than anyone else, and then don't be afraid to spread the word.

Is your company REAPing the benefits of social media marketing campaigns? Or is it sitting idly by, watching as more and more of its competitors hop aboard this cutting-edge business transition that has revolutionized the way that consumers respond to companies and their products? The social media marketing train is about to leave the station, and if you don't jump on board now, you almost assuredly will be left behind. So take the time to learn about Web communities like Twitter and Facebook, at all times watching how social media–savvy companies are communicating and interacting with their consumers. Then take a leap of faith and join up with those platforms that are the best fit for your brand's marketing needs. Leverage these social media sites to your advantage. Use them to project the essence of your company, your products, and your message loud and clear across cyberspace, and provide your consumers with the tools that they need to spread the good word about your company to others. After all, if you're not speaking up about your company, who else might be doing so? And just what might they be saying?

I'm not implying that your company is engaged in any manner of sordid dealings or has done *anything*, really, to elicit negative feedback. But just think about how many times you have sat in the coffee room with your colleagues, bad-mouthing the food at so-and-so's restaurant or the service at so-and-so's retail store. Now try to think back to the last time you discussed with a friend over lunch just how *fantastic* a new product that you just purchased is. The latter of these two thought exercises is a tad more difficult, now, isn't it? Here's why: people just can't *wait* to share their bad news with others, so it travels fast, furiously, and frequently. Good news, on the other hand, takes time to mature and is communicated to others mainly at their request. Which brings me back to my original questions: If you're not speaking up about your company, who else might be doing so? And just what might they be saying, in all likelihood? (Cue ominous music.) But let me go against the grain and offer up a piece of good news: social media networks have stepped in as grand equalizers, leveling out the speed with which bad news and good news are circulated. Sure, bad news still can travel at neck-breaking speeds, zipping around the Internet from site to site faster than you can say "patchouli." But now, *so can good news*—even when it's not solicited.

Your products and your store's message, as fantastic as they may be, are no longer adequate means of counteracting the bad-mouthing blather that plagues every company, nor are they very effective tools for motivating your consumers to purchase. So, step up, leverage the phenomenon of social networking, develop a marketing program that broadcasts the story that you want others to tell about your company and products, and influence the influencers. And don't forget to make it easy for your core customers to become ambassadors of your brand. Pinpoint the exact message that you want them to relay, and then script their role as influencers. Tell them what to say. Arm them with an arsenal of reasons that their friends or families should purchase your unique products and not anyone else's. And when your core consumers bring you business, reward them. After all, giving them a $50 discount off their bill—or even just a free cup of coffee—is a small price to pay to hook a new customer for life.

Somebody Help Me

If you've ever been in the market for some new home products, then you probably are familiar with IKEA, the Swedish retailer that offers flat-pack design furniture for incredibly affordable prices. But no matter how great this home goods retailer's price tags are—take, for example, its Lack coffee table, which retails for just $39.99—the IKEA experience is not for the faint of heart, to say the least. First of all, IKEA warehouses often are located in suburbs just outside major urban centers, so for city dwellers who rely solely on public transportation, the prospect of even traveling to these blue and yellow buildings is daunting. Then, when consumers finally do step foot into their local IKEA, they discover that the only way to walk through its three- to four-floor showroom is to follow a one-way path that winds and ambles its way past every one of the thousands of pieces of home goods IKEA has to offer. And say they find an item that they want to take home with them. They can't pick up the item then and there, where they see it on the sales floor. No, instead they must traipse through the rest of the store, following the predesignated path that has been laid out for them, until they reach IKEA's self-serve section, where they must locate the flat-pack boxes containing the items they would like to purchase and then load them onto dollies.

The IKEA adventure doesn't end there! Once consumers lug their purchases back home, they are faced with the task of interpreting 10-page-long instruction manuals—none of which contain written instructions, mind you, only pictures—and assembling their furniture by themselves. The comedian Hal Sparks has been attributed with a joke that *perfectly* sums up the IKEA experience: "My day was terrible. I spent six hours on the phone with IKEA technical support. It was six hours of this: 'Um, can I speak to someone who isn't Swedish? Yes, I was assembling the Klorn entertainment center, and I've become trapped inside!'"

Not many consumers today have the patience—or the fortitude—to stomach everything a trip to IKEA entails, and given how the rules of consumption have changed, it's no surprise. Many a consumer has evolved from an approach of DIY (Do-It-Yourself) into DIFM (Do-It-For-Me), and who else is leading the transition's charge but baby boomers? After all, as these consumers are aging, they are finding that they just don't have the muscle for all the heavy lifting that is involved with DIY anymore. They won't *admit*, mind you, that they're not the strapping young lads and lasses they once were. But nevertheless, they are aging and frankly just don't have the strength to accomplish the projects that they might not have hesitated to tackle on their own in their younger days. What's more, many boomers have reached a stage in their lives where they are financially secure enough to pay someone else to do the job for them, someone who will do it once—and do it right. By footing the bill for a service technician or a skilled laborer to take care of a project, boomers avoid the frustration and additional expense that often come with undertaking the job themselves.

I can certainly understand why former DIYers would decide to eschew their old, enterprising ways and become DIFMers, and I understood why even more so after I decided to take on the job of repairing a leak in the irrigation system of a newly purchased home. I set about to my task, measuring out some copper pipe, fitting it where I believed the source of the leak to be, and soldering the pipe into place. Then I tested the water pressure. Guess what? Another leak popped up. So I repeated my process all over again, but this time at the source of the new leak. I tested the water pressure again, and yet *another* leak sprang to action. No kidding, this happened no less than *seven* times. I continued mending and testing, mending and testing, until finally I mended all but the last segment of the irrigation system's copper piping. I tested the water pressure, and yes, there still was a dripping leak in the final section of piping that couldn't be ignored. So one last time, I measured and cut the pipe, soldered it into place, brushed my hands off, and realized that I had replaced *an entire irrigation system's worth of piping*. Of course, it was only after I had repaired the leakage that I learned that the previous owner of the home had failed to drain the full length of copper piping the previous winter. Water had frozen in the system, creating weaknesses and splits in almost every elbow of piping in the entire irrigation system. Now, wouldn't I have been better off to just hire a professional to do the job for me instead of taking multiple trips to the home improvement store, shelling out dollar after dollar for putty, copper pipe, piping elbows, and soldering butane, and spending hours cutting and fitting and soldering until the system finally operated properly? I know that boomers sure would think so!

Figure 13.1 shows the percentage of baby boomers who make it to the home improvement store to do it yourself; as you can see, it is steadily decreasing. No doubt they're finding someone to do the job for them.

Even if you are an experienced pipe layer and DIYer, who might not have much sympathy for my travails with the irrigation system, there must be *some* project out there that isn't exactly your forte. For example, how savvy are you when it comes to restoring your laptop to factory settings, or setting up your surround sound system so that it syncs with your television, your DVD player, *and* your stereo? Even if you are a tech whiz (what *can't* you do?), the introduction of so many new technological advances and gadgetry

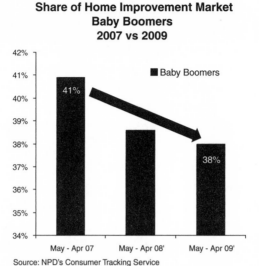

Share of Home Improvement Market
Baby Boomers
2007 vs 2009

Source: NPD's Consumer Tracking Service

Figure 13.1   Do it yourself or do it for me.

into today's world of consumption has made it increasingly more difficult for many consumers to keep pace with the rate of change. In fact, when I conduct consumer interviews in electronics stores, the majority of the shoppers tell me that they are in the store to begin with only because they need help hooking up their new products. True, most products do come with setup manuals, but their instructions are just not as easy to follow as both the manufacturers and consumers might hope they'd be. For many consumers, these guides might as well be written in a foreign language, *that's* how confusing they are.

In recognition of the fact that so many of their customers are simply baffled by technology, some electronics retailers have risen to the occasion, offering in-home setup services as well as tech support centers that answer users' questions 24 hours a day, seven days a week. But as consumers quickly realized, not all retailers' service centers are cut from the same cloth. And if you think that a second-rate tech support team won't break a business, think again. Consumers have their pick of a litter of electronics stores that provide tech support services, so why would they turn to a retailer with a subpar tech team for their purchases if another store serves up exactly the kind of help that they need? Just look at Best Buy as compared to what happened to Circuit City. Hordes of consumers to this day swear by Best Buy's tech support team, dubbed the Geek Squad, and even cite it as the differentiating factor that leads them to shop at this particular retailer. Circuit City's Firedog techies, on the other hand, were, shall we say, less than successful. Now, I'm well-aware that Circuit City eventually went under due to a number of complicating factors, but it certainly wouldn't have *hurt* its business at all if its Firedogs had been able to provide the same level of customer service that Best Buy's Geek Squad offers. After all, Best Buy has the strong, loyal consumers that it does today principally because its friendly, knowledgeable Geek Squad provides them with the security that comes with knowing that an entire team of experts will be there to help them through whatever electronics problems they might experience. And today's DIFM consumers really do place a high premium on companies and brands that will protect their passions—or at least be there to help them get their passions back up and running smoothly again!

DIFMers also appreciate retailers that can take the grunt work— like delivery and installation—out of the shopping equation for them, which is yet another area in which Best Buy excels. Now, I know that I already exonerated Best Buy once in this chapter, but this is just one brand that seems to have a firm handle on customer service, so let's proceed. Think back to the holiday shopping season of 2008, when retailers across the board were selling similar if not exactly the same products as both their higher- and lower-level competitors. As I was scanning various retailers' circulars one week during that holiday season, I noticed that two stores, Wal-Mart and Best Buy, were offering what appeared to be the exact same product—a Samsung 50-inch plasma television—but for two different prices. When I looked a little closer, I saw that Wal-Mart's television, which sold for $958, was listed as model number PN50A400, whereas Best Buy's television, which sold for $1199.99, was listed as model number PN50A450. "Why the difference in price and model number?" I wondered. After all, these two televisions *looked* exactly the same. So, determined to figure out what specific differentiating feature Best Buy's version included that would justify its more expensive price tag, I performed a side-by-side comparison of the two televisions. I checked the product description of each, the number of channels each provided, the pixel count of each, and I even pored through the fine-print specifications of each. And do you know what? I couldn't find even *one* difference between the two sets.

As it turns out, the difference was nothing consumers would ever notice. That is, until they actually purchased the television from one of these two retailers. If consumers purchased the television from Wal-Mart with the goal of saving money, a store employee would walk them out to their cars and help them load the enormous, boxed-up television into their trunks—if it actually *fit*. But consumers who purchased the television from Best Buy, on the other hand, would get it delivered to their door, along with a trained Geek Squad technician, who would calibrate the set to their exact specifications. Of course, the techie also would make sure the darn thing worked properly! So even though it seemed like the only real distinguishing factor between Wal-Mart's television and Best Buy's was price, the true customer service difference was like night and day. And for those of you thrifty critics out there who are thinking, "Hey, don't just gloss over the price difference! For $250 extra dollars in my wallet, I'd be happy to lug the television back to my house and figure out how to get it set up!" get this: if consumers brought Wal-Mart's advertisement for the Samsung 50-inch television into Best Buy, sales associates would match Wal-Mart's price—even with the discrepancy in model numbers. How's *that* for customer service?

Best Buy is one of a handful of retailers that understands what fewer and fewer brands today do: that customer service, when it is executed conscientiously, is an art form that can provide companies just the edge on their competition that they're looking for. After all, consumers no longer view good customer service as an expendable quality in the retailers that they frequent. No, they want—nay, *demand*—good customer service, and if you don't have it, you'd better believe that your consumers will happen upon another brand out there, perhaps even one of your competitors, that will give it to them. And heaven forbid the consumers discover that one of your competitors offers consistently fantastic customer service, because in that case, you'll have lost them for life. Your competitor's service will foster a sense of loyalty in your straying consumers, and there are few determinants in the purchasing equation that will break the bonds that service forges.

"Yeah, yeah," I hear you skeptics saying. "We've got customers who have been loyal to us for *years*. Our customer service is just fine the way it is, thank you." Well, a word of warning for you cynics out there: as more and more DIYers grow older and transition into DIFMers, customer service will become more important to consumers than it has ever been before. Just ask the elderly gentleman whom I met at Home Depot. I asked this older man what he was shopping for, and he told me that he was in the market for a new dryer. He had even pinpointed the appliance that he thought was right for him, and had ventured into Home Depot to see if it carried the model that he was looking for. As we got to talking, the elderly gentleman mentioned to me that Home Depot was not the first store he had visited that day. As it turns out, he had just come from a competitor down the road, but he had left that store in disgust after experiencing what he considered terrible customer service. I asked him to explain what it was about the competitor's service that was so bad, and he turned to me and said, "What service? No one wanted to help me at all. I wouldn't call that *service*."

He then went into further detail and informed me that rather than actively seeking out customers in need of assistance, the sales associates at the previous store had just stood around, waiting for customers to approach them with their questions. Finally, the elderly man was able to track down an employee to help him out with his very simple query. He had merely wanted to know how much in total he would have to pay to buy the unit that he was planning on purchasing. The sales associate quoted him a price that was about $20 higher than Home Depot's, and then mentioned that he would be charged an additional $49 in delivery, setup, and haul-away fees. That was the last straw for this older gentleman. Not only did he have a heck of a time rooting out a sales associate to answer his question in the first place, but now this particular retailer was actually going to *charge* him for a service that he knew he could easily find elsewhere for free! The elderly man did what any other consumer would have done in the same situation: he said, "Thanks, but no, thanks," then hopped into his car, drove down to Home Depot, and purchased the dryer for $20 less than what he would have paid at the first retailer—with a whole lot better customer service to boot.

Home Depot was at the ready when the elderly gentleman implored, "Somebody help me!" and I sure hope your company will be too when your consumers make the same appeal. After all, the difference today between making a sale and not making one, between retaining consumers and losing them, and even between staying in business and folding is, you guessed it, customer service. So, don't lose sight of this great differentiator, lest your competition sneaks up on you from behind and matches—or, worse yet—beats you at the service game. And don't cut customer service corners, either. Sure, it may be more cost effective to set up self-service counters, like the beauty industry has done, and let your consumers wade through the sea of your product offerings until they find what they hope is the right product for them.

It may be easier on your sales associates to loiter in the aisles of your store until they are approached by a confused consumer. But when you leave your consumers to their own devices and don't actively attempt to talk them through their purchasing decisions, how will they be able to understand which of your products best fits their needs? How will they be able to appreciate the essences of your offerings? In order for a product to sing to consumers— not just talk, or even whisper, but truly *sing*—the product must tell a story. And it is up to you to do its talking.

PART 3

THE NEW BRAND

CHAPTER 14

Tip-Top Tech

How would you like to sell one million units of your product in just one month? How about in one week? What, you don't think it's possible? Then how do you explain the fact that Apple iPhone 3G 16GB, which sold at the steep price of $299, did?

As Figure 14.1 illustrates, in the worst economy in over a decade, Apple's iPhone 3G stirred a frenzy of consumer desire, despite its high price tag. In fact, some news outlets reported that eager shoppers had lined up in front of Apple's Fifth Avenue retail location in New York City no less than one week prior to the product's launch, just so they would be one of the lucky few to take an iPhone 3G home with them on the first day that it was available for purchase. Yes, you read that correctly: they waited *one whole week*! Outside! In the oppressive heat of a Northeastern summer! Just to buy a cell phone!

Well, to be fair, as consumers worldwide all know by now, the Apple iPhone is not just *any* cell phone. It is the cream of the crop, the smartest of smart phones, the most technologically advanced of all tech products—which is exactly why it has sold so well. After all, it's no secret that technology is a major driving force behind consumer desire today. Consumers want the products that they buy to represent the progress that is happening all around them. They view technology not as a luxury, but as a value-add, and products like the iPhone, which integrates a score of technological functions into one palm-sized gadget, fit perfectly into consumers'

Apple iPhone 3 GS Sales

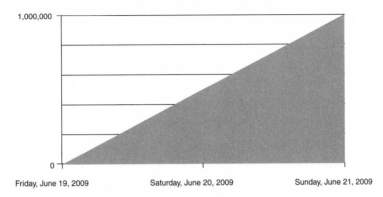

Figure 14.1 Sales of Apple's iPhone 3G for the first three days on the market.

value equations. Sure, there are tried-and-true, iconic products. Some things are just best left untouched. But unless your company manufactures Eames lounge chairs or duct tape, you will need to begin approaching your products with the spirit of innovation if you want to keep your consumers engaged. While it's true that your company might be more comfortable staying stuck in the same old mold, in the same old place it always has been, the time has come for you to unhitch your business from the ways of the past and leap onto the cusp of the cutting edge of technology. Who knows? If you do so effectively, you may just walk up to one of your retail stores the week before a major product launch to find consumers camped out in preparation for what you have to offer. And even if this never happens, take heart in the fact that your willingness to provide your consumers with the technological advances that they so unanimously desire will position your company for successes it may have never deemed imaginable.

For example, who among us would have bet money on the fact that an automobile brand like Hyundai would join the ranks of Lexus, Porsche, and Cadillac as one of the best-ranked cars for quality? I'm sure Hyundai never would have. That is, until it began listening to drivers' desires. And, boy, did it listen. It heard that drivers wanted the kind of advanced technological luxuries that generally are found in $60,000 automobiles. It heard that drivers were drawn to automobiles that feature in-car gadgets, like movie screens and stereo-integrated MP3 players. It heard that drivers placed a high premium on enhanced reliability, external and internal styling, fuel efficiency, electric engines, and hybrid automobiles. So Hyundai gave them all that, and it did so for a heck of a lot less money than Lexus, Porsche, or Cadillac ever would. And then, to top thing things off, Hyundai even began offering its consumers a 12-month complimentary assurance program when they finance or lease a new car, which allows consumers to return their Hyundai to their local dealer without further financial obligation should they lose their job or experience a life-altering medical impairment. It's no wonder, then, that during the abominable retail environment of 2008–2009, when Ford, General Motors, and Chrysler were losing sales at a rate of over 25 percent per month, Hyundai was able to show just a minor loss as compared to its last-year sales. After all, Hyundai had heard the consumer. Hyundai had heard, listened, and responded. And so did the consumer.

Now, your consumers won't always be vocal about their tech needs, but that doesn't mean that you should merely wait around for them to speak up. After all, *you're* the expert of your products. You know better than anyone else the kinds of emergent technologies that can be integrated into your offerings. You appreciate better than anyone else just how talented your product designers are. You understand better than anyone else what appeals to your target demographic and what doesn't. In fact, there is no one person better positioned to lead the charge of technologically advancing your products than you. So, what are you waiting for? Anticipate your customers' needs and desires, develop an item that they didn't even know that they needed, and take their engagement in your products to the next level.

Nintendo was able to do this quite literally when it introduced its Wii gaming console to the retail marketplace. Before the Wii burst onto the scene in 2006, the gaming experience was fairly standard: gamers would pop in a game cartridge, recline in their most comfortable chairs, and then give their thumbs the workout of a lifetime as they maneuvered their video game character of choice from level to level. But little did these gamers know that while they were sitting in their living rooms and exercising their thumbs, Nintendo was quietly developing a game console that could give their *entire bodies* the workout of a lifetime. You see, instead of strategizing ways to improve the graphics or online gaming capabilities of its preexisting consoles, like other video game manufacturers had been doing, Nintendo decided that it was time that the world was introduced to the first truly interactive video game system—the Nintendo Wii.

Featuring an avatar editor that enables gamers to create video game versions of themselves as well as the Wiimote, a motion-sensing controller that allows users to interact with and control on-screen items with gesture recognition technology, the Wii gets gamers off the couch, on their feet, and moving. For example, if a gamer wants to play Wii Tennis, she inserts the disc for the Wii Sports video game into her game console, stands back from the screen, and swings the Wiimote like a tennis racket whenever the ball is lobbed to her side of the court. Now, how's *that* for product engagement? Indeed, because Nintendo has leveraged the abilities of its staff, its knowledge of the gaming industry, and its ability to anticipate gamers' needs and desires, it has been able to develop a revolutionary new product that has engaged consumers like never before. Just ask all those gamers out there suffering from tennis elbow!

While consumers always appreciate industry-exploding technologies like the Nintendo Wii, sometimes infusing even a small dose of technology into your products can make a world of difference to them. Take, for example, how enthusiastically beauty consumers responded when Lancôme introduced its Ôscillation mascara, which features a built-in vibration system in its handle. Indeed, consumers gobbled up these $36 tubes of mascara, which apply product more thoroughly and evenly in the same or even less time than traditional, manual brushes do. In fact, consumers have been so enamored of Lancôme's new offering that in no time at all, Ôscillation mascara has become the second-best-selling beauty product in department stores. Now, if only someone would invent slippers with little vibrating motors inside. Can you say "Happy Feet"?

You might be thinking, "But there is no *way* that my company can begin developing technologically advanced products. In fact, our products have nothing to do with technology whatsoever!" Well, to you, I say, "If a beauty company could do it, *then so can you.*" Sometimes introducing even the smallest of technological advancements into your preexisting product offerings can transform them from ordinary into extraordinary. And if you have absolutely no idea where to begin, don't be afraid to look to industries outside your own for inspiration. That's what Lancôme did. To be sure, a whole host of vibrating, pulsating, and otherwise buzzing products, from massaging razors to electronic toothbrushes to cell phones, hit the market far before Ôscillation mascara ever emerged. Ultimately, of course, the decision to incorporate technology into your product offerings is up to you. But remember that fantasy we discussed earlier on in this chapter? The one about consumers waiting for days on end in a line that wraps its way around an entire city block just to purchase your newest product? Well, I can almost guarantee that you can kiss that dream goodbye if you don't at least consider capitalizing on the consumers' soft spot for technology.

Luxury: A Tiffany Moment

Here's a thought exercise: Imagine I have in my possession two items, one of which is an envelope containing a $75 gift card from Target and the other a Tiffany Blue Box, which is tied up nicely with a white ribbon. Now, because I'm a generous man, I'm going to give you one of these two items. Yes, that's right: simply choose one of these items, and it's yours. Should you go with the Target gift card? After all, Target has just about every product offering under the sun, and 75 smackers could go a long way. Or should you go with what's inside the box? Tick tock, tick tock, tick tock . . .

Time's up. So, which item did you choose, the Target gift card or the Tiffany Blue Box? If you're like most people, you chose the Tiffany Blue Box. What if I told you that the item in the box is not worth as much as the gift card? Would that change your mind? Again, if you're like most of the people whom I have actually led through this exercise in person, you'll *still* choose the Tiffany Blue Box. Why is that? As far as I can tell, the very experience of seeing and opening that little blue box elicits an almost palpably emotional response in most people. They untie the white satin ribbon. They carefully lift the lid off the box. They run their fingers over the blue felt pouch with the Tiffany & Co. insignia scrolled across it. And then, they open the pouch, and in it is a silver pen. And they are absolutely *thrilled*. It doesn't matter to them that the pen costs $65 at full price—$10 less than the Target gift card. No, not after they've had a "Tiffany moment." All that matters to them is that they now have in their possession an item from none other than *Tiffany*, whose very name evokes luxuries beyond most people's imaginations.

Consumers definitely do have a soft spot for luxury, and in the years leading up to the economic collapse of 2008–2009, it seemed that luxury could do no wrong. Consumers of all income levels and age brackets were reaching well beyond their means to purchase all kinds of luxury goods just so they could share in their own little way in the wealth that the economic boom of the 2000s had brought to so many. Indeed, every consumer demographic, from the poor to the middle class to the rich, from teens to young adults to boomers, shifted its purchasing priorities from pure necessities to needs and eventually to desires until finally soaking up the life of luxury. And retailers and brands, always happy to provide consumers with more, more, more, began offering consumers the more expensive product lines that they so desired.

Exponential growth was the rule, not the exception, for companies that successfully catered to consumers' craving for luxury items. Some retailers and brands were even posting double-digit growth for their comparable store sales, thanks to the big bucks that consumers were spending—or should I say charging to their credit cards—on every luxury item imaginable, from automobiles to apparel and from electronics to electrolysis. Yes, luxury was on a roll, and consumers were gobbling up big-screen televisions; front-load washer and dryer sets; professional-grade, stainless-steel appliances; leased luxury automobiles; bigger homes; furniture bought on time with no interest payments for a year; handbags the size of a football field; jeans retailing for the price of a week-long cruise; the newest electronics on the market offering the latest and greatest features . . . *phew*! Shall I go on? I'll spare you the roll call, but consumers purchased all of these items and more without any regard for how they would finance them and with every desire in the world to own them.

To say that the luxury market flourished under the weight of all of the consumer dollars that were flooding into it would be an understatement. More accurately, it inflated so much that its growth became unsustainable. Indeed, even though the luxury market was one of the last sectors to be affected by the economic tsunami of 2008–2009, it eventually was hit—and hit *hard*, with a blow that was perhaps even harder than that any other industry had been dealt. To make matters worse, luxury had been so busy enjoying the fact that its consumers were spending with reckless abandon that it had failed to notice the economic storm clouds that were gathering in the distance. And when these clouds opened up and bombarded luxury with tightened credit markets, shrunken bank accounts, a vulnerable stock market, and consumers' unwillingness to shop, it was all that the luxury industry could do to come up for air.

Luxury has swum its way out of the worst of the economic downturn of 2008–2009, but it has yet to fully recover because it is still relying on the bad habits it developed during, shall we say, happier times. But no longer will simply stitching a designer name onto the tag of a $400 pair of jeans pass as luxury. The days of logo slapping are over for now. Instead, brands and retailers will have to find a way to return to the golden age of justified luxury, of luxury that feels so special, so unique, so best in class that it lavishes a Tiffany moment upon consumers. They will have to infuse such a level of luxurious association into their names that their products create instant connections with consumers. They will have to shower consumers with *pure* luxury, luxury for the utter sake of luxuriousness. And they will have to provide consumers with products that are customized to match their every need, whim, or desire—items that are not one of a million, but rather one *in* a million.

Indeed, more now than perhaps ever before, luxury consumers want the *real deal*. They want the inimitable item that sets them apart from every other consumer out there, the handbag that they *know* none of their friends owns, the dress that they *are positive* that no one else at the cocktail party will be donning, the briefcase that they *are confident* no other man on the train will be carrying … I think you get my point. Just think about it for a moment: have you ever approached a friend, complimented her on her necklace, asked her where she purchased it, and received the following response: "Oh, *this thing*? I picked it up in Laos while I was traveling on business." "Yeah, sure you did," you mutter to yourself, disgruntled that she's being so proprietary with her information. I mean, after all, it's just a *necklace*, right? Well, sure it is. But not to her, it's not. To her, it's the product that distinguishes her, the item that completes her style, the accessory that projects exactly the image she is aiming for. Of course, I can't vouch for your friend. I can't say for certain that she actually bought her piece of jewelry in Laos. But what I *can* say is that she sure as heck doesn't want to look like everyone else. And neither would you.

So, why not leverage consumers' desire for customized, personalized, one-of-a-kind—or even one-of-a-very-few—luxury products that are in a category all of their own? The process of doing so could be as simple as limiting the production run of one of your high-end items, which ensures consumers against the possibility of running into one of their neighbors at the grocery store who is wearing the exact same luxury watch that they are. What about offering to etch an engraving into one of your products? Apple does this to great success with its iPods and iPhones, as does Tiffany, which extends to customers the option of engraving a wide range of its products, including necklaces, money clips, cufflinks, and baby rattles. Or how about going above and beyond and inviting your customers to design one of your products to their exact specifications? Take NikeiD Studio, for example, which is an innovative, by-appointment service that gives consumers the opportunity to visit one of the two NikeiD Studio retail locations in New York City and consult one on one with Nike designers in order to customize a pair of footwear that perfectly reflects their own unique styles and personalities. By encouraging its customers to not just join in on but rather drive the design process of their footwear, Nike transforms what ordinarily might be merely an average, everyday purchase into a luxury item that is unique to its customers and to them alone. And as anyone who has actually designed a pair of sneakers at a NikeiD Studio knows, when customers finally are shipped the shoes that they spent hours laboring over to get the color combinations and materials just right, the experience of receiving and opening up their custom-made creations is akin to a Tiffany moment.

With so many available options to up the ante of your luxury items, what measures are you going to take to fulfill your customers' desire for their very own Tiffany moment? How are you going to set your product or brand apart so that it is readily identifiable to consumers as the apex of luxury? How are you going to draw the kind of excitement out of consumers that makes them squirm with anticipation at the prospect of even unwrapping your products' packaging? How are you going to captivate consumers to such an extent that they will choose your brand or product over another of even greater value? And how are you going to communicate to consumers what it is that makes your products or brand so very special? Here's a hint: the idea of wrapping your products up in a little blue box with a white satin ribbon is already taken. Regardless of what you decide to do, remember that while luxury has found its way into the hearts of many consumers, it has lost its way into their wallets. So remind consumers why it was that they grew so fond of luxury goods in the first place. Furnish them with exquisite, high-quality, one-of-a-kind products that they won't be able to purchase from anyone other than you. Equip your products with the kind of luxuriousness that sings to consumers. And if you're successful, the Tiffany moment might just be renamed after you.

A Little Bit of Privacy Please!

Have you ever ventured into a JCPenny store and browsed through its clothing racks? If you have, perhaps you've stumbled upon a line dubbed American Living, whose offerings include everything from argyle sweater vests to graphic tees to little black dresses to classic polo shirts. If you're like me, when you first set eyes upon this particular collection of clothing, you might have thought to yourself, "Now, there's something familiar about these clothes. I can't quite put my finger on it, and I'm fairly certain that I've never encountered this label prior to today, but I *know* that I've seen these all-American, Nantucket-style clothes some-where else before." Well, allow me to let you in on one of the worst-kept secrets in the fashion industry: as it turns out, you probably *have* seen these items before, albeit in slightly different variations, because the designer behind JCPenny's American Living collection is none other than Ralph Lauren.

The American Living line of clothing is just one of several sub-brands—otherwise known as private labels—that Ralph Lau-ren designs. In fact, Ralph Lauren offers just under *30* different private brands today, including Black Label, Collection, Polo Ralph Lauren, Polo Golf, Polo Denim, and Lauren Jeans Co. Heck, it even has a Ralph Lauren Paint label! But why in heaven's name does Ralph Lauren think it needs nearly 30 dif-ferent labels? What would be the possible benefit of breaking down its product offerings into so many sub-brands? Actually,

the answers to these two questions are really quite obvious—
that is, it is if you take a moment to ponder just how wide a spec-
trum of consumers is drawn to Ralph Lauren's unique perspective
on fashion.

Without a doubt, consumers across all income levels are attracted
to Ralph Lauren's high-end preppy polo shirts and tweed blazers—
but not all of them can afford to shell out $145 for one of its but-
ton-up shirts. No, the only items that lower-income consumers
would button up after stepping into a Ralph Lauren retail location
and glancing at a few price tags would be their pocketbooks. So, in
an effort to meet the needs and desires of both their potential and
actual consumers, the team members that have made Ralph Lauren
into the industry icon that it is thoughtfully asked themselves,
"What else can we possibly do to entice all of our would-be customers to purchase from us? How can we shift our product offerings so that they align with what consumers really want and need?
Is there a way we can cater to all the consumers that want to take
part in the Ralph Lauren experience while still maintaining the pres-
tige of our brand?"

The team members thought long and hard, and then, finally,
inspiration struck them: *private branding.* Indeed, Ralph Lauren's
team members found that if they used "good, better, best" selling
to create price-differentiated private brands, ranging from their very
expensive Purple Label to their downright affordable, JCPenny-
exclusive American Living line, they could cast Ralph Lauren's net
over consumers in almost every socioeconomic bracket without tar-
nishing the high-end reputation of the brand. Yes, you read that
correctly: this high-end designer has created nearly *30 different
brands*, all in an effort to open up the adventure of shopping at and
purchasing from Ralph Lauren to just about everyone who feels the
desire to do so. And, boy, how consumers have responded! To be
sure, now the only items that lower-income consumers are button-
ing up after visiting their local department stores are their newly

purchased, utterly affordable pieces of clothing from Ralph Lauren's lower-priced private brands.

While Ralph Lauren's preferred style of differentiating its private brands on the basis of tiered price points may be relatively new to the retail world, the overriding concept of private labeling is by no means a recent sales phenomenon. Indeed, if Barney Kroger, the eponymous founder of the Kroger supermarket chain, were alive today, he'd proudly tell you that in the 1930s he stocked the shelves of his grocery stores with homemade sauerkraut housed in old-fashioned packaging to boost his stores' margins. But while Barney certainly was a true pioneer of private branding, even he would agree that the art of developing and managing private labels and brands has come a long way over the course of the past century. The type of homespun private labeling that Barney helped spearhead in the 1930s transitioned into a more hands-off style of private branding by the 1970s, when retailers began asking wholesalers and factories to produce generic, no-frills commodity products for their chain stores. And by the time the 2000s rolled around, the private labeling game had advanced to the next level. As the preceding example of JCPenny and Ralph Lauren demonstrates, various brands and value-oriented retailers today have joined forces to develop unique, complex approaches to dispatching their private brands into the retail marketplace. Their hope, or course, is to differentiate themselves from the competition and expand the scope of their products' reach. And while not all companies are so enthusiastic that they have integrated 30 private labels into their overall business game plans in order to reach a wider demographic of consumers—*ahem*, Ralph Lauren!—many brands and retailers today nevertheless are harnessing this sales vehicle to great success.

Just look at how eagerly consumers worldwide have welcomed Wal-Mart's private brands into their homes. Wal-Mart's Ol' Roy private label dog food, named after founder Sam Walton's faithful hunting companion, has become the most successful seller of all dog food brands in the United States, and its Great Value and Equate products are so well received that they are shelved in its stores worldwide. Consumers also have had an overwhelmingly positive response to the exclusive branding partnerships that the chain retailer has forged with a number of iconic fashion industry and celebrity personalities, including country pop sensation Taylor Swift and renowned fashion designers Norma Kamali and Mark Eisner, all of whom develop products just for Wal-Mart. Indeed, thanks to its ever-widening array of private brands, which provides its consumers with product offerings ranging from higher-end, high-design goods to low-cost, everyday items, Wal-Mart has been able to shuck off its former reputation as a second-rate discount retailer and has emerged as a top go-to shopping resource for price-savvy consumers worldwide.

But Wal-Mart won't be crowned the top discount shopping destination just yet—not if Target, yet another major chain retailer that has demonstrated a mastery of the art of private labeling, has anything to say about it. To be sure, Target is giving not just Wal-Mart but *all* chain retailers a run for their money because of how successfully it has been able to synthesize private brands into its overall range of product offerings. Avid home decorators don't simply take leisurely strolls through this major retailer's home department. More accurately, they gasp with excitement, then run from aisle to aisle as they uncover not only Target's very own home furnishing lines, like Modern Home, Xhilaration, and Circo, but also dozens of products that have been developed exclusively for Target by some of the most legendary names in home fashion, including Michael Graves, DwellStudio, Thomas O'Brien, and Victoria Hagen.

Similarly, female shoppers are hard pressed to survive a trip to Target without caving in and buying at least one of the many clothing offerings that have been created specifically with them in mind. After all, given that these female consumers have the option of purchasing from within Target's low-priced Merona store brand, its

GO International program, which features clothing from an ever-rotating selection of emerging fashion designers, and its Converse One Star for Target label—among many other private brands—how could they *not* go home with something new? And don't even get me started on how thoroughly Target has revolutionized the concept of privately labeled cosmetics! Target's line after private line of superbly designed yet still affordable goods has demonstrated just how dedicated it is to the task of providing "Design for All: Great design. Every day. For everyone," as one of its advertising campaigns so accurately trumpets. And in turn, consumers of all income levels and fashion sensibilities have demonstrated just how dedicated they are to what Target has to offer.

Private labeling certainly is a bona fide sales technique that allows retailers and brands to expand the span of their reach by providing consumers at all income levels the low-cost, high-quality products that they desire. But this sales strategy need not always be employed by businesses as a means to drive *down* the prices of their merchandise. Indeed, when retailers and brands develop their own privately labeled products that are store exclusive and not carried elsewhere, they are able to administer more control over when, to what extent, and even *if* they discount these items than they would if they were selling the exact same labels or brands as every other retailer in the marketplace. After all, if your store stocks a privately labeled brand of products that can only be found on your shelves, then there is no way that your competitors can undersell you on these items, simply because they do not even *carry* the same lines of merchandise that you do! So, let's say that you sell designer jeans, and one of your competitors decides to discount its stock of 7 For All Mankind denim. Well, all those apparel retailers that also carry 7 For All Mankind jeans will be forced to mark down their prices as well, lest they lose momentum, sales, or even customers. But you? You don't need to worry about discounting your offerings before you are ready to, because you were smart enough to collaborate with a denim designer and create an altogether new line of privately labeled jeans that are exclusive to your store. No, you can wait to mark down your denim selection, and you can do so using your own set of criteria—not because your competitors' discounted prices drove you to do so.

Private labeling is certainly a powerful tool that retailers and brands alike can wield to their advantage, but that doesn't mean that it doesn't come with its fair share of hazards. To be sure, consumers will not flock to a retailer simply because it stocks a massive assortment of products. Consumers are looking for variety, yes, but they don't have the time or the patience to weed through masses and heaps of offerings before pinpointing the products that they need and desire. So, provided you decide to expand your product lineups by incorporating privately branded merchandise into your range of offerings, remember that your privately labeled products will stand out from their pure branded competitors only if you orchestrate your efforts shrewdly and with an inordinate degree of precision. For example, let's say that your store is planning on releasing its own privately branded lineup of socks, and to kick off the campaign, you assign your product developers the task of designing every kind of sock imaginable for your new product line, from anti-odor, moisture-managing socks right down to basic athletic and business socks. But, wait a minute: do your stores *really* need a privately branded version of basic socks? Think about it: how many brands of socks that offer plain old basic socks does your store already stock? Hanes socks, Pro Feet socks, Jockey socks, Gold Toe socks, Champion socks, Rite Fit socks, TravelSox socks . . . and I'm sure the list continues. Then, why bother introducing yet another brand of basic socks to your shelves that consumers will be forced to sift through until they find the pair that is right for them? Instead, brainstorm a way to set your privately labeled socks apart from every other brand that is currently crowding your shelves. Inject a quality into your privately branded products that cannot be found anywhere else. I don't care if you have to use polka dots or engineer massaging socks to do so. Just find a way.

Private labels and private brands are fully engaged in the combat for consumers that is raging currently in the retail marketplace, and if your brand or company has yet to implement private labeling into your overall business strategy, the time has come for you to wrap your hands around this powerful sales vehicle and brandish it to your advantage. So, raise the product bar by introducing high-quality, competitively priced private brands to your inventory. Get ahead of your pure branded competition by utilizing private labeling to take control of the pricing game. And give your consumers a little privacy—that is, *private branding*.

Turning Adversity into Opportunity Tips

Allow me a moment of sentimentality before we embark upon the final chapter of our journey together. After all, I feel almost like a high school teacher who, in the closing days of the school year, finds himself impelled to pass along a few words of parting advice to his senior students before they head out into the great unknown. Now, don't worry. I'm not going to start quoting lines from Dr. Seuss's *Oh, the Places You'll Go!* But I would be remiss if I sent you off into the new retail reality without equipping you with a tool belt of tried-and-true tips for you to leverage as the need arises.

The following 22 tips are pulled directly from the presentations and motivational sessions that I deliver to clients and companies who are looking to understand how to better market their products in today's new retail environment. As retail continues to evolve, so too will these tips. Some will fade in, and others will fade out. Some will remain of the utmost importance for far longer than others will. And there's always the possibility that retail will shift sharply yet again at some point in the near future, necessitating that several of these tips be thrown out the window and replaced by fresh ones. Fortunately for you, however, I post new tips to NPD's Web site at http://www.npd.com every few months, so be sure to check that site frequently to stay abreast of the trends that are driving the retail marketplace. You also can reach out to me directly with any questions or requests you may have through NPD's Web site by navigating to http://www.npd.com/beyondthedatalive/. I'm just a hop, click, and a jump away.

Now, without further ado, I present to you my tips for turning retail adversity into sales opportunities. May you use them prudently—and profitably.

THINK COLOR

Do you remember my renowned Bloomingdale's sweater wall that I described in Chapter 8? It exploded with every gradient of colors imaginable, and it popped so vibrantly that it grabbed even the president of Bloomingdale's eye. Or perhaps you recall from that same chapter how effectively Nautica wielded color to its advantage in its outlet location in Hilton Head, South Carolina? No sales tactic employed by any other retailer at that outlet mall was able to draw me into its store as quickly as Nautica's expert use of color did. Or maybe you can even call to mind the Lowe's commercial for its Valspar brand paint? In the advertisement, a husband and wife are shown in the paint aisle of a Lowe's retail location. As they deliberate over which colors might fit their walls best, a Lowe's paint technician informs them that green paint exerts a very calming effect on a home. The camera then cuts to a shot of two wild and rambunctious young children running circles around their home. The young duo bounds up the stairs, disappears into their bedroom, which has been newly painted "Spring Meadow" green, and then . . . silence. The kids' bewildered parents, who are putting the final touches on the children's bedroom walls, slowly turn around only to discover that their high-energy children are now quietly sitting down in the back of the room, reading *Pride and Prejudice* and *Sense and Sensibility*. Color strikes again!

To be sure, color holds court over consumers. It can grab their attention before the styles—and certainly the prices—of your products do. It can lead them by the nose directly into your stores. It can subconsciously pull on their psyches to such an extent that it shifts their very moods from agitated to serene, from apathetic to engaged. It can even entice your consumers to buy more of your products than they otherwise would. For example, picture the following scenario: One day while you're shopping, you happen upon a shirt. But this particular shirt is not like every other shirt out there. No, this shirt is *the shirt* for you. It fits your physique perfectly and your sense of style even better. Now, imagine that the store that carries this particular shirt offers it not just in one color but in *five*. Odds are that while you might not buy the shirt in all five colors, you'll probably buy more shirts than you otherwise would have had it come in only one color.

I'm not suggesting that you should offer every single product that you carry in every one of the seven colors of the rainbow. But when you're looking to cut your inventory in leaner economic times, don't take the sizzle of color out of your assortment mix. After all, when you give your consumers color, you give them a new reason to buy. So think of color as your friend, as something that separates your products from those of the competition, and your bottom line may find out just how calming of a color *green* can be.

RIGHT SHADE OF GREEN

Since we're already on the topic of green, consider the impact that the environmental movement has had on consumers worldwide. Indeed, just before the global economy collapsed in 2008, there was no other topic that consumers wrung their hands over more than "going green." Once content to simply toss their banana peels out of the windows of their cars, consumers all of a sudden began Googling "How to Compost at Home" and buying special worms to munch up the grounds from their morning cup of coffee. Okay, maybe that's a bit of an exaggeration, but my point remains: consumers will shell out copious amounts of green just to become more, well, *green.*

Before you begin to strategize ways to capitalize on consumers' growing eco-fondness, bear in mind that the green movement has lost some of its momentum since the economy took a turn for the worse and diverted consumers' attention away from the health of the environment and onto that of their 401(k)s. But even though the green movement has browned out a bit lately, I predict that we will see it rise yet again as frugal consumers weigh the cost benefits of buying, for example, one eco-friendly compact fluorescent light-bulb with a seven-year warranty for $3.99 versus one standard incandescent bulb with a two-month-long life expectancy for the same price. As it turns out, environmentally sustainable products are savvy investments not only for the planet but also for consumers' checking accounts, and I fully expect the green marketplace to begin sprouting once again as soon as the economy stabilizes—yes, pun intended.

Consumers also are developing a keener interest in products that emit what I like to call a different shade of green, thanks to the philanthropic tie-ins that are built into the purchasing process of these items. Also referred to as embedded giving, this sales strategy entails promising consumers that a certain percentage of the money that they pay for a specific product will be donated to a charitable cause. Think about the various companies, including Gap, Apple, Converse, and American Express, that have joined forces with (RED), an organization dedicated to providing anti-retroviral medication to AIDS sufferers in Africa. These brands develop exclusive (RED) products or services that fit within their existing offerings and then donate up to 50 percent of the proceeds from the sales of these items to (RED)'s cause. Or what about Paul Newman's philanthropic association, the Newman's Own Foundation, which donates 100 percent of its net royalties and profits after taxes from the sale of Newman's Own food and beverage products to charity? Now, I would bet that you're probably not quite ready to surrender 100 percent of your proceeds to charity—not yet, at least. But do keep in mind that consumers often are willing to spend more on products that allow them to give back in some way, shape, or form to the world around them. So find the shade of green that flatters your company best and wear it proudly for all your consumers to see.

PRICE TIERING

Some brands today have been able to successfully adapt to the less-than-predictable buying habits of today's consumers by utilizing multitiered sales strategies. Some call this style of selling "good, better, best." Others simply refer to it as premium-level producting. But no matter its name, it involves offering consumers varying price tiers of the same or similar products in an effort to connect with as many segments of the shopping public as possible—and when executed correctly, it happens to be extremely effective.

Just look at how enthusiastically consumers across all income levels have responded to the automobile industry's efforts to expand the scope of its product offerings. In an attempt to entice lower-income consumers to purchase or lease their high-end automobiles, carmakers like BMW, Mercedes, Volvo, Audi, and Land Rover have begun to offer entry-level car options that can be written into almost any budget. Similarly, car companies that traditionally have been associated with lower- to mid-income consumers have developed higher-end sister companies, like Toyota's Lexus, Nissan's Infiniti, and Honda's Acura, in order to furnish higher-income consumers with luxury cars that they so desire. And although these automakers' preferred method of product tiering involves creating entirely separate classes of vehicles, differentiating between your good, better, and best merchandise need not be so complicated. Sometimes utilizing even a simple relabeling or rebranding campaign to split hairs between your offerings can work just as effectively as developing altogether new grades of products. But no matter what tiering tactic you decide to put into play, don't forget that there's a whole world of shoppers out there, from aspirational consumers to just plain affluent ones, and it is up to you to create a range of products that calls each and every one of their names.

PRODUCT DIFFERENTIATION

Today's consumers are thrifty, yes, but that doesn't mean that they don't appreciate a unique product when they stumble upon one. But how are you going to position your products so that shoppers can't help but pick them up when they're digging through the thousands of offerings on retailers' shelves? What are you going to do to ensure that your merchandise sings to consumers louder than that of any other manufacturer? If your company hasn't yet determined the answers to these questions, it's about time that it did. After all, when a consumer visits her local pharmacy in order to purchase a bottle of shampoo, for example, she doesn't care that your company offers moisturizing shampoo. "Big whoop," she thinks, "a million other beauty supply companies sell moisturizing shampoo." But if she sees that your company's shampoo not only will moisturize her hair but will do so using all-organic materials, well, then, *that's* a different story. And even better, if she notices that both your company and one of your competitors offer all-organic moisturizing shampoo but that your version of the product is less expensive, guess whose shampoo she will be more inclined to buy? You guessed it: yours. So cater to consumers' desire for difference. Create products that are not one *of* a million but rather one *in* a million.

RELEVANCE

Bills, bills, and even more bills seem to be the major concerns that are weighing on consumers' minds—and their bank accounts—these days. First they have to ante up their incomes on their mortgage or rent payments, then they are tasked with putting money down on their phone and Internet bills, and then of course they need to cover the cost of incidentals, like drug prescriptions and, oh, yes, food! To be sure, consumers of all stripes are spreading their hard-earned cash so thinly that once they finally pay off all of their recurring expenses for the month, they are left with little discretionary income for any purchase that is even a smidgeon less than necessary. So, how are you going to prove to consumers just how essential your products are? Demonstrate to them how much easier their lives can be with your products by their side. Help them justify their purchases by providing them with merchandise that is as relevant to their needs and lifestyles as can be. And cut through the cobwebs of concerns in their minds by clearly communicating that relevance to those consumers to whom it speaks to best.

TECHNOLOGY

No matter whether your company deals in electronics, appliances, beauty products, automobiles, apparel, or some other category of merchandise altogether, it is up to you to keep pace with consumers' ceaseless desire for the most technologically advanced products. Sure, tried-and-true merchandise certainly has its place on retailers' shelves, but given that even paper towel manufacturers and carpet shampoo companies are finding ways to integrate technology into their product offerings, do you really think you can afford to sit back and relax while the rest of the retail world passes you by? Consumers today want—nay, *expect*—their products to do more than ever before, so tune your company's attention toward innovation, and let technology lift your wares from good to great.

NEW AND IMPROVED

Speaking of innovation, when was the last time that your company performed a full-scale upgrade of its product offerings? Now, I'm not asking you how long it has been since you touched up your logo or revamped the packaging of your products. After all, "change for the sake of change" does not in any language translate to "new and improved." And at any rate, consumers can sniff out the difference between a true, justifiable enhancement versus a cosmetic, packaging "upgrade." No, what I want to know is when did you last sit down and analyze your products, determine what implementable tweaks would improve them, and then set out to actuate those updates? One year? Three years? Ten years? No matter how much—or how little—time has passed since your last product overhaul, consider taking a page from Apple's product playbook.

Apple by no means *needs* to upgrade its iPod at the rate at which it does. Indeed, even after the original iPod had been on the market for a full year, there *still* was no other MP3 player that could hope to compete with Apple's be-all, end-all portable music player. In fact, to this *day* no other product compares. Apple nevertheless stays one step ahead of the competition at all times by releasing a new edition of its iconic iPod on an almost yearly basis, before the previous version has even lived out its full life. And wouldn't you know it, whenever Apple unleashes a brand new generation of iPods into the marketplace, consumers who already own fully functional iPods can't help but think to themselves, "*Maybe*, just *maybe* I should update this old thing." Don't you think it's about time that maybe, just maybe, your consumers updated their older versions of your products? I, for one, certainly do. So, think new, and by all means, think improved.

BUILD THE CORE FIRST

Nothing says management efficiency to me quite like a company that is able to remain focused on its core business. But the sad fact of the matter is that companies like this are becoming more and more difficult to come by. Indeed, "Grow, grow, grow, by any means necessary" seems to be the mantra of many companies today, who are more eager to acquire smaller brands or reach outside of their core areas of expertise than they are to nurture the key elements of their business. And almost without fail, these growth-greedy companies eventually veer off course, expose the vulnerabilities of their brands' core elements, and lose all understanding of what it means to deliver innovation to the marketplace.

Take UGG, the shearling boot company, for example. Five years ago, UGG tried to expand its product offerings into women's sportswear and began dishing up down parkas, toggle sweaters, and even swimwear cover-ups to what it thought would be a ready and eager shopping audience. Well, UGG thought wrong. Its women's sportswear collection didn't take off in quite the manner that it projected, and to make matters worse, UGG spent so much time refining its new line of clothing that it lost sight of how to compete in its core outdoor boots business. Eventually, the company was sold to a footwear conglomerate, which had the wisdom to bring the brand back to its core and encourage UGG to rediscover its roots. And that UGG did. The footwear company quickly set about to refocusing its efforts on its core product and began a full-scale expansion of its footwear assortment, a move that ultimately brought the brand back to life and elevated UGG to all-new heights. UGG had to go full circle to realize that it should have been concentrating on its core business all along, but you by no means need to do the same. Learn from this footwear company's missteps and refuse to fall prey to the alluring yet distracting charms of growth. Keep to your core, and growth will naturally follow.

LEAN AND MEAN

From time to time, brands and retailers are faced with the task of cutting back their inventory. You should know this as well as anyone. You may have been confronted with this particular responsibility yourself at one point in time. So, how did you approach your cuts? Did you excise your basics, shredding those products that give you steady but muted sales so that your top-selling products could be given top billing? For your sake, I hope not. Sure, I understand the logic of paring back only those items whose sales seem lackluster in comparison to your best-selling products. Only produce what is most productive, right? Well, not quite.

Think of the situation this way: Pretend you own an ice cream parlor. Year after year, your top-selling flavors are vanilla and chocolate. You can't keep these two flavors in stock, actually, *that's* how quickly consumers are buying vanilla and chocolate ice cream cones. So you think to yourself, "Geez. Why do I even bother carrying other flavors? I sell more chocolate and vanilla ice cream cones in one day than I sell of the other flavors in a week's time. I should really cut back my inventory of those other flavors." And that you do, opting to offer only chocolate and vanilla ice cream to your consumers. But then, low and behold, a competitor opens up shop across the street from your parlor, and he offers *three times* the amount of flavors that you do. And now, the consumers that once came to you for their ice cream cones decide, "Hey, this new parlor not only serves up chocolate and vanilla, but it also carries four other flavors of ice cream that I can try out should the mood strike me. I'm eating my ice cream here from now on."

I think you understand my point: yes, you need products that buzz, items that you *know* that consumers are hankering for. But if you only serve up the sizzle, you can rest assured that consumers will turn elsewhere for their more conventional purchases. When what your consumer wants is a simple T-shirt but all that you sell are tube tops, she really has no other option but to head to a different store, does she? So find the right balance of the basics, or volume-oriented products, and sizzle, or merchandise that will grab your consumers' attention and spark their interest. After all, chocolate and vanilla just aren't enough to satiate even the paltriest of consumer appetites these days.

PASSION IS CRITICAL

Do you remember the woman with the insatiable zeal for handbags who I wrote about in Chapter 8? She had no less than 30 different styles of bags holed away in her laundry room, yet still was convinced that she needed the newest tote that Michael Kors had to offer. She had a passion for handbags, alright, and she certainly is not the only consumer whose purchases are driven by such an intense amount of fervor. Indeed, different consumers feel acute emotional connections to different goods, and regardless of what type of products you offer up to the buying public, be they fishing lures or umbrellas, the odds are in your favor that there is a faction of shoppers out there who is just as drawn to your wares as the Michael Kors fan is to handbags. So why not play to consumers' passion and let them know just how in synch your products are with their needs and desires? Why not communicate to them, with both your offerings and your marketing messages, how deeply you understand their commitment to your products? New Balance was able to successfully tap into the passion that fuels the workouts of both hard-core and wannabe runners alike with its love/hate advertising campaign, which leveraged the torrid relationship that these athletes have with their sport. The footwear company assured its consumers that it appreciated that running is "a constant balance, a balance between joy and pain, work and play, a balance between love and hate," and in doing so spoke directly to the emotions that impel runners up and out of their warm beds every day for their morning jogs. Now, the question remains: how are you going to speak to your consumers' passion?

COMFORT AND WELLNESS

For over a decade, the comfort and wellness movement has been gathering steam slowly, quietly, and ever so surely, and several industries already have begun to cater to consumers' growing desire to eat healthy, feel healthy, and be healthy. The beauty business, for example, was one of the first sectors to expand its emphasis from simply looking better to ultimately feeling better as well. Companies within the food industry, too, have met with great success when they create products that are specifically designed to enhance consumers' well-being. Take Glacéau Vitaminwater, for example, a beverage company that manufactures and distributes 15 different kinds of naturally flavored, water-based drinks that are infused with everything from vitamins A, C, and E to ribose to theanine. And if you're not sure what beneficial effects ribose and theanine have on the body, well, neither does 95 percent of the consumers who buy these drinks, but that doesn't stop these shoppers from purchasing Vitaminwater! They figure they'll drink one down a week, just in case it *is* effective, all in the pursuit of good health!

Just imagine all the different ways you can play the comfort and wellness card to your advantage with your current product offerings. Do you work in the automobile industry? No problem! Simply design car seats with built-in lumbar support cushions that are easy on drivers' backs. Do you deal in footwear? Why not put your production team to work on a pair of shoes that literally gives wearers an added bounce to their steps? How about those of you who are involved in the fashion industry? Wouldn't it be great if yours was the first company that offered a pair of jeans that could help consumers lose weight just by wearing them? Or what if your

213

company was the first to the market with a bra that massages women's shoulders all day? Now, I'm sure some of these would-be products may sound far-fetched, to say the least, but it wasn't so long ago that consumers would have scoffed at the idea of drinking a beverage that is enhanced with vitamins. So keep your mind open to the hundreds upon thousands of comfort and well-ness product possibilities that are just waiting to be explored. And if you steal one of my ideas, hey, at least give me a little bit of credit!

THE NEW DEAL

Retailers are throwing all manner of fantastic deals to consumers today in an effort to entice less-than-intrepid shoppers into their stores, but many of these merchants have lost sight of the fact that discounted prices and buy-one-get-one-free promotions are not the only bargains that fit squarely into consumers' value equations. After all, what real benefit do stores derive by slashing their prices by 50 percent or more? Sure, these deals may help retailers unload some of their excess inventory, but at what cost to their bottom lines? Similarly, what good is a buy-one-get-one-free promotion when the product consumers are buying is a refrigerator? I, for one, don't know of too many shoppers who need, let alone *have room for*, two refrigerators!

The time has come for retailers to begin offering an altogether *new* kind of deal—one that pairs nicely with their consumers' existing needs and desires and that may even end up costing less in the long run. So, say you are considering holding a promotion to persuade consumers to purchase a specific model of desktop computers that you offer. Now, you could simply discount these computers by 20 percent to ensure that inventory moves through your store quickly. Or, you could take a moment to think about what kinds of products might combine well with your computers, like printers or sets of peripheral speakers, and then bundle these items together in a package deal. What if you are preparing to release a new plasma television to the market, and you want to extend an introductory deal for consumers who are quick to the purchasing punch? Why not throw in a free DVD player to those shoppers who buy your television within its first month on the market? There are hundreds of ways to configure the new deal so that it fits your offerings to a tee, so find the path that's right for you and your products, and you just may find your consumers tagging along for the journey.

DISCOUNT DETOX

Now, I know I just trumpeted the benefits of incorporating new deals into your selling strategies, but I urge you to leverage this and all other product promotions only at your utmost discretion. Don't get me wrong: when I'm on the buying side of the equation, I appreciate a good discount just as much as the next shopper. But consumers today have grown too accustomed to these markdowns, have come to expect them, and postpone purchasing an item until a discount incentivizes them to do so. So, if you ever want to see the sun rise on a day when the majority of your products are sold at full price, you have no other option but to put your consumers on a healthy regimen of Discount Detox.

Begin the weaning process by offering products that are so compelling, so passion inducing that consumers have no recourse to still their yearning but to buy these items immediately. Consider limiting the amount of products that you release into the marketplace to teach procrastinating purchasers the hard lesson that if they don't buy today, they may not be able to do so tomorrow. Delay discounting your merchandise until you absolutely cannot stall any longer. And then, painful step by painful step, consumers will begin to adjust to the new retail reality that you create for them.

DESIRE VS. NEED

Once content to pull out their pocketbooks and purchase as their passions dictated, consumers today have drastically curtailed their spending and are shopping on an as-needed basis. But when did retailers concede defeat and begin acquiescing to the fact that purchases today are more planned than they are impulsive, are more rational than they are emotional, and are more practical than they are desire driven? Just because economic times are tough doesn't mean that the fire that previously fueled consumer spending has been completely and utterly extinguished. No, look closely and you will see that the latent flames of purchasing passion are slowly corroding consumers' newfound frugality. So, stoke the blaze. Remind them how good it feels to lust after and then obtain the objects of their affection. Reassure them that indulging every now and then won't break their budgets. And entice them to purchase your products by stirring up their memories of how sexy, rewarding, and beneficial it is for them to do so. The embers of consumers' desire are just waiting to be ignited, so strike a match and watch their purchasing pleasure explode.

LUXURY

Recall the thought exercise that I led you through in Chapter 15, wherein I told you that out of the goodness of my heart, I would hand over to you either a $75 Target gift card or a Tiffany Blue Box, complete with a white satin ribbon. The choice was altogether yours. Or was it? While the pragmatic part of your brain might have poked you in the ribs and said, "Pick the gift card! At least you know how much it's worth!" there was something holding you back from doing so, wasn't there? That *something*, that little voice in the back of your head that was rooting for you to select the little blue box, was nothing other than your inherent soft spot for the kind of pure luxury that retailers like Tiffany & Co. have been successfully lavishing upon their consumers for years.

If, as I suspect, you found yourself drawn to the little blue box, take heart in the fact that you're certainly not alone in your enthusiasm for the type of luxury that Tiffany represents. Indeed, as I noted in Chapter 15, the majority of consumers today would have made the exact same selection that you did when confronted with the choice of a quantifiable $75 Target gift card or a box that is the embodiment of luxury for the pure and simple sake of luxuriousness. And if yours is a company that caters to consumers who lust after luxury, I suggest that you take a page from Tiffany's playbook and present your consumers with the types of luxury items that are so finely crafted, so best in class, so unlike anything else on the marketplace that consumers can't help but justify spending exorbitant amounts of money on them. After all, consumers just don't have the kind of free cash or credit anymore to spend on luxury purchases that are anything less than, well, *luxurious*. Gone are the days of false luxury, when high-end designers could get away with charging luxury prices for their products simply by swathing them in repeating patterns of their companies' logos. So, consider how your company is going to return to the golden age of luxury, when luxury items outclassed every other product on the market. Think about how you're going to infuse your luxury items with such a high level of quality and craftsmanship that consumers will be helplessly romanced back into the folds of luxury. And offer consumers the type of products that will elicit the Tiffany moments that they so desire.

DRAMATIC CHANGE

It was not long ago that the fashion industry distinctly defined for consumers which styles were hot and which were not so hot. Indeed, the latest fashion trends were once so abundantly apparent that women wouldn't dare step outside in long skirts after short skirts had popped up on designers' runways in Paris, New York, and Milan. But the clear demarcation of what's in and what's out grew decidedly blurrier somewhere around the turn of the twenty-first century, when fashion retailers and brands decided that consumers wanted more leeway with their wardrobes and began offering "transitional" apparel that could stand the test of several fashion seasons' worth of time.

Consumers initially responded enthusiastically to the new pieces of transitional apparel that were making their grand entrances on sales floors and in window displays of fashion retailers worldwide, and designers high-fived one another for the fantastic boon in fashion sales that their concept had prompted. But then, a funny thing happened: the huge upswing in transitional apparel sales that the fashion industry had been so thoroughly enjoying suddenly began slowing down, then slackened to a mere trickle, and eventually petered out altogether. "What could have possibly gone wrong?" designers and retailers alike wondered. "Consumers were wild about transitional apparel just two months ago!" As it turned out, consumers *were* wild about transitional apparel. In fact, they were *so* wild about it that in no time at all they had stuffed their closets to the brim with these articles of clothing, whose nearly timeless styling eliminated the need for consumers to venture out to the mall in search of the latest fashions. After all, who needs to wrack up charge after charge on their credit cards for the newest, hippest styles of clothing when anything goes in fashion, when consumers can wear long skirts or short ones, when they can wear pants or suits or even dresses, when far more items are in style than are passé, and when few if any styles ever reach the point of obsolescence? The truth is that *no one does.* Indeed, as fashion designers quickly learned, by introducing transitional apparel to consumers' closets, they effectively eliminated from their product offerings the element of dramatic change, which is essential to driving sales in the fashion equation.

Dramatic change is not only vital to promoting sales within the fashion industry. To be sure, sectors across the board are faced with the task of implementing dramatic change into their product lineups to tempt consumers, who are preprogrammed to desire the latest, most stylish, most technologically advanced items on the market, to purchase their latest offerings—and many are doing so to great success. Just look at how effectively companies within the electronics sector, like Apple and Sony, have leveraged dramatic change to their advantage. These companies update and reinvigorate their offerings with such frequency that consumers, in an attempt to keep pace with the ever-increasing rate of dramatic technological advancements, often will purchase a new television or stereo system years before their models at home have lived out even half of their product lifespans. You might just say that electronics has outfashioned the fashion industry! Or consider how adeptly footwear designers have applied dramatic change to their product lineups. In 2007, high heels tore up the fashion runways, and consumers rushed out to purchase heels in every shape, size, color, and pattern. Then, in 2008, flats emerged as the must-have fashion accessory of the year, and once again, consumers set out to their local retailers and bought up heelless shoes in every fabric, hue, and design imaginable. Come 2009, footwear designers threw consumers for a loop yet again and introduced six-inch heels to the marketplace, and, well, by now I'm sure you can guess how consumers responded.

So, look to imbue change into your product offerings—and not just any old change, but *dramatic* change. If you work in the automobile industry, don't merely alter the headlight shape of your cars;

remodel their entire bodies. If you manufacture handbags, don't simply jazz up one of your preexisting totes with a buckle flap here and a new print there; craft an altogether new bag that is unlike anything else on the market. If you are in the home furnishings industry, don't just release your bookshelves and desks in new colors; conceptualize wholly new product designs that will push your older offerings into obsolescence. Grow dramatically. If you do so, you might just see your market share grow dramatically as well.

GAME CHANGER

Think with me for a moment, and think hard: can you recall an MP3 player that predates the Apple iPod? I sure can't, and with good reason: when Apple released its first generation of iPods onto the electronics market in October 2001, it achieved what no other electronics manufacturer had yet to accomplish and transitioned MP3 players from nice-to-have products into must-have items. Yes, the Apple iPod changed the MP3 game, alright, and in doing so forever altered the way that people interact with and experience music, but its iconic portable music player isn't the only game-changing product that Apple has introduced to wide consumer acclaim. Just ask those consumers with Apple iPhones if they could revert back to the older clamshell phone models they once used, and their response will be a resounding "No, absolutely not!" Now, of course these consumers *could* still survive without their trusty iPhones in their pockets, but the point is that they don't want to. After all, the iPhone has changed the way they approach their day-to-day existence so much so that they have grown dependent upon these devices, and depriving them of their trusty handheld sidekicks would be the equivalent of forcing an addict into rehab.

Indeed, no matter whether they are intended for education, entertainment, or business purposes, Apple's high-design, technologically superior electronics have revolutionized the way that consumers go about their lives. It matters not to Apple fanatics that Apple's products often are more expensive than those of its competitors, nor are they particularly miffed that Apple retail locations sometimes are hard to come by. No, these consumers focus on how much better their lives are made by Apple's state-of-the-art electronics, attentive customer service representatives, knowledgeable support staff, and incredibly easy-to-use products, and they remain loyal Apple addicts to their graves.

Even if yours is not an industry that readily lends itself to innovative breakthroughs, take heart in the fact that companies of all stripes constantly are finding ways to become game changers. Once upon a time, for example, consumers were forced to schlep their suitcases over their shoulders as they ran from airport terminal to airport terminal in their rush to board their connecting flights. Then one day it dawned on luggage manufacturers: let's place *wheels* on our suitcases! As anyone who has been to an airport recently would attest, even this incredibly simple concept has exerted an enormously positive impact on travelers worldwide. So, strategize how you can transform your offerings in a way that will transform your entire industry, and watch your products resonate with consumers in a whole new light.

EDUCATE AND COMMUNICATE

Is there anyone else in the world who knows your products better than you do? What about your brand's message? Does anyone out there understand what sets your company apart from its competitors better than you do? I doubt it, which is why it is up to you—and you alone—to loudly and clearly communicate, communicate, communicate the essence of your company, your products, and your message to your consumers.

Whether you utilize tried-and-true communication tactics, like direct-to-consumer advertising, or employ more technologically advanced methods of consumer outreach, like social media marketing campaigns, is entirely your choice. What is no longer your choice, however, is simply relying upon retailers and other third parties to broadcast the benefits of your products to your consumers—or, worse yet, leaving your consumers to their own devices to educate themselves about what it is that you have to offer. As I mentioned in Chapter 13, the only way for your brand and your products to truly sing to your consumers is if you give them a voice. So, test your vocal chords, clear your throat if you need to, and muster up the loudest shout you can to ensure that your company's messages resound with consumers across all four corners of the earth.

LIFESTYLE EVOLUTION

In my previous book, *Why Customers Do What They Do*, which was published in 2006, I expounded upon the benefits of lifestyle marketing, describing the then-revolutionary sales tactic in the following way: "Consumers today are more interested in brands from companies that understand their complex lifestyles. It is not enough to market your brand to a specifically targeted consumer. The interests and needs of consumers, along with their distractions, have grown at huge rates, and your brand must measure up to all these elements to succeed." Now, let's say that you picked this book off the shelf today and thought to yourself, "Hey, why don't *I* apply lifestyle marketing to my bicycle manufacturing company's sales strategy?" And that you do, deciding to kick off your efforts to sell the entire biking experience to your consumers by conceptualizing new items to add to your product lineup, including not only various gradations of cycles, ranging from premium to downright cheap, but also bike helmets, shirts, pants, shoes, CamelBak hydration packs, and replacement bicycle parts.

But, wait! Before you take one more step, scratch that sales approach, my fearless reader! While consumers may have demanded back in 2006 that one solitary brand furnish them with every single product they could possibly desire, their tastes have shifted, as they always, inevitably, do. Indeed, consumers today have grown weary of retailers and manufacturers bombarding them with scores upon scores of mediocre product offerings. No, they don't have the time or the patience to sift through a veritable deluge of items in order to pin down what it is that they are actually looking for—which is simply the best of the absolute best products that a brand has to offer. So, why waste your bicycle company's time and energy—not to mention that of your consumers!—on expanding into product offerings that you know are not your strong suits? Instead, think about evolving from lifestyle marketing to *pinpoint marketing*, which involves singling out those items among your range of products that your bicycle brand is best known for and then redirecting your sales efforts onto only those things. For example, perhaps your bicycle manufacturing company has little to no experience in developing helmets, but it *does* design a mean, lean, aerodynamic, carbon fiber-framed cycling machine. Well, then, focus your sales attention on your top-of-the-line bicycle, and leave bike helmets to experts like Louis Garneau. After all, if you stick to that which you do better than all the rest, today's consumers will be more inclined than ever to stick by your brand's side.

FOFI AND LOFI

For those readers out there who have dabbled a bit in accounting, the title of this particular sales tip is not a typo of FIFO (First In, First Out) and LIFO (Last In, Last Out)—nor do you need to worry that I am about to test you on what, exactly, those specific accounting methods actually entail! No, when I reference FOFI sectors, I am referring to those industries that were among the first to collapse when the economic tsunami of 2008–2009 struck the retail marketplace and are poised to be among the first to rebound from it—First Out, First In. Similarly, when I reference LOFI sectors, I am referring to those industries that were among the last to succumb to the financial crisis yet are poised to be among the first to recover from it—Last Out, First In.

The following are a few examples of some FOFI and LOFI industries:

FOFI	LOFI
Real estate	Handbags
Furniture	Footwear
Home décor	Sporting goods
Home improvement	Sunglasses
Appliances	Watches

Contrary to what you might think, I bring up FOFI and LOFI sectors not to give you nightmarish flashbacks to your Accounting 101 final exam in college. Rather, I do so because if your company happens to operate within either a FOFI or LOFI industry, or those sectors that consumers will first redirect their purchasing attention to as soon as the smoke from the financial crisis clears, it is imperative that you prepare yourself for the looming consumer spending surge that will soon assail your company. Now, you may think that the most prudent course of action you can take is to let the whole economic mess sort itself out before you even begin to consider ramping up your inventory, refocusing your marketing efforts, or expanding your product offerings. But don't forget that consumers have spent a full year eyeing items and services that strike their fancy, breathlessly anticipating the day when they feel comfortable enough to splurge again on the products that they so desire—and that day is rapidly approaching for those companies in FOFI and LOFI industries. So, if your company happens to fall within a FOFI or LOFI industry, you had better pull out your rain boots and umbrellas and brace yourself, your company, your products, and your sales strategy for the impending spending storm. And if you don't? Well, you can rest assured that when consumers regain their spending confidence and begin snatching up the products that they have lusted after for so long, your brand will be left out in the rain.

DEMO OF DEMOGRAPHICS

Let's say that you are a salesperson for an automobile maker, and your supervisor assigns you the task of identifying the characteristics of your primary demographic of consumers. "Easy as pie!" you think, then quickly jot down what you deem to be the top three descriptive qualities of your consumers: male, male, male. Well, I have three words for you: wrong, wrong, wrong. Just because men were the primary purchasers of automobiles yesterday does not mean that they will remain in that top spot tomorrow. In fact, just because *any* particular demographic of consumers was your primary purchaser yesterday does not mean that it will be tomorrow. Indeed, traditional consumer demographics as the marketplace once knew them are changing before retailers' very eyes. So, don't fall into the trap of assuming that those consumers with the power of the purchase are the same shoppers who once constituted your traditional target market. If I have said it once, I have said it a thousand times: the winds of the purchasing game are a-changin', my friend, and it is up to you to lift up your wings and fly right along with them.

PRICE NO LONGER PRIMARY: THE NEW VALUE EQUATION

If you were to take a stab at the number one reason consumers choose to purchase the products that they do, you probably would select price, wouldn't you? If so, you certainly wouldn't be wrong. Yes, low-cost items *do* have their allure, and I would be lying if I told you that the majority of consumers don't place a high premium on products whose stickers feature bargain bin prices. But while low ticket prices play a very important role in consumers' value equations these days, shoppers today are weighing far more factors than just price as they migrate into the new economic world of consumption. Indeed, value for today's consumers takes all manner of forms, from brand recognition to quality and durability, from customizability to luxuriousness, and from serviceability to overall desirability. Heck, for some consumers the difference between a valuable product and an expendable one comes down to eco-friendliness, healthfulness, and even country of origin. So, play to your consumers' desire for value and imbue qualities into your merchandise that they can't find in any other product—*especially* the lowest-priced option on the shelf. And then, help them understand just how valuable your products are by clearly communicating their worth to the retail marketplace.

! ! !

We have reached the culmination of our journey together, and the 22 tips that I have laid out for you in this chapter will form the groundwork for you to follow as you proceed along the path to growth. You need not follow each and every suggestion that I have presented. Perhaps you even will choose to pay no heed to any of my tips. But before you do so, ask yourself:

Do I want to finish the race, or do I want to *win* the race?
Do I want to play, or do I want to *compete*?

If you chose the latter of the two options in the preceding questions, then even one or two of my tips might create just the right balance you, your company, and your products need to succeed in today's challenging economic environment. And before you venture out into the new retail landscape, don't forget: balance takes risk, and risk yields rewards.

CONCLUSION

You and I have undertaken quite a journey together as we've progressed through the pages of this book. Yes, we have pioneered our ways across the frontier of the new retail landscape and in the process discovered just how greatly the economy, consumers, and even brands have changed since the onset of the 2008–2009 global recession. We have ascertained what, exactly, you and your company can do to adapt to these ongoing shifts in the retail environment so that you emerge from the economic downturn stronger and better positioned to entice your consumers to choose your products and ignore the rest than you have ever been before. What's more, we have even pored through a veritable avalanche of lessons, tips, tools, tidbits of advice, case studies, NPD market research, and recommendations that were designed to help you manage your company, your brand, and your products through today's tough consumption times, including:

- The characteristics of frugal fatigue, wherein consumers grow weary of denying themselves the pleasure of purchasing for months on end

- How to slash your inventory so that it is lean and mean, not lean and, well, *boring*
- How color and assortment are the spice of life and can entice consumers to purchase multiple variations of the products that you carry
- How essential it is to keep up with the ever-increasing pace of technological advancements, no matter what your industry or product category is
- How to keep an open mind when you are innovating your products, always raising the bar higher and higher with each new item that you release onto the marketplace
- Not to change for change's sake, but rather for your *consumers'* sakes
- The importance of maintaining your focus on the integrity of both your core products and your core business
- The difference between lead, need, and deed consumers, and what you can do to influence the buying behaviors of all three categories
- The hazards of discounting your products, and how essential it will be for retailers to subject their consumers to a strenuous regimen of Discount Detox
- How to tap into consumers' value equations so that your products perfectly align with their specific needs and desires
- The great extent to which passion drives consumers to purchase, as well as how to leverage consumers' emotions to your advantage
- That your company will only REAP what it sows, so make your products **R**elevant, **E**xciting, and **A**ltering, and use **P**inpoint marketing to do so

If your company experiences difficulty adjusting to the various marketing and selling dictums that have arisen during the new era of consumption, take solace in the fact that you're not alone.

Indeed, retailers and brands across all manner of industries have spent so much time and energy trying to navigate their ways out of the wreckage of the 2008–2009 recession that they are at a loss as to how to keep pace with consumption's ever-changing rulebook. No, I won't pretend that it's easy to formulate fresh approaches to marketing and selling to all of the various demographics of consumers that might purchase your products when you are out of kilter; it's all that you can do to even regain the right balance of product offerings and growth in your business. But regardless of how trying the process of adapting to the new retail landscape may be, it is crucial that you do so. It is time to do the following:

- Create new traditions
- Ignite passion in consumers
- Innovate your message, your products, your packaging, and even the system by which retailers deliver their merchandise to consumers
- Discover new ways to educate consumers
- Recognize that success is measured by a new yardstick

Seeing your company, your brand, and your products through this new era of consumption history is an art form all its own, but now you are prepared to take on the future of retail and create a masterpiece of your own designs.

INDEX

Note: Boldface numbers indicate illustrations.

ABOUT THE AUTHOR

Marshal Cohen chief industry analyst of The NPD Group, Inc., is a nationally known expert on consumer behavior and the retail industry. He has followed retail trends for more than thirty years, at NPD and as the head of leading fashion and apparel companies as well as major retailers. As part of his work at NPD, Marshal leads many top firms in long range and strategic planning sessions. He often utilizes motivational presentations to help launch corporate goals and kick-off meetings.

In addition to his duties at NPD, Marshal is currently a guest professor at North Carolina State University, School of Textiles. There he is introducing students and faculty to techniques for analyzing and applying data. Recently, Marshal has been a guest lecturer at the Fashion Institute of Technology and at the Wharton School of Business.

Marshal is also a regular contributor to many major media outlets. He is frequently quoted in publications like *The Wall Street Journal*, *The New York Times*, and *Women's Wear Daily*. Additionally, he appears on various television news programs including

Today, Good Morning America, CBS Sunday Morning, and is a regular guest on Bloomberg TV and Fox Business News. He is also a sought after speaker at key industry events such as MAGIC and Sourcing at MAGIC, The WSA Show, The Fairchild CEO Summits, The National Retail Federation's (NRF) Annual Convention, and The American Apparel and Footwear Association's (AAFA) Annual Convention.

Since joining NPD in 1999, Marshal has held a variety of positions analyzing and interpreting NPD's uniquely combined consumer and point-of-sale tracking services for the apparel and footwear industries. Marshal was born for this role, and has been in retail since he was 7 years old and worked in his father's store in New York City. As fate would have it, he returned to retail while in college studying law. He started by working part-time at Bloomingdale's and was then selected to be part of their training program. Over the subsequent 10 years he moved up through the ranks to buyer and ultimately merchandise manager. His career progressed and took him into the wholesale and manufacturing end of the fashion business. He eventually headed up designer brands such as WilliWear, Stanley Blacker, and Adrienne Vittadini. He was also the founder, owner, and president of Motive Marketing Group.